850 FREE-MOTION QUILTING DESIGNS

Encyclopedia of Continuous-Line Patterns

Stitch Pictorial Motifs & Allover Textures

Laura Lee Fritz

C&T PUBLISHING
Another Maker Inspired!

Text copyright © 2025 by Laura Lee Fritz

Photography and artwork copyright © 2001, 2002, 2008, 2011 by C&T Publishing, Inc. and Laura Lee Fritz

PUBLISHER: Amy Barrett-Daffin

CREATIVE DIRECTOR: Gailen Runge

EDITORS: Madison Moore, Gailen Runge, Stacy Chamness, Cyndy Lyle Rymer

TECHNICAL EDITORS: Sara Kate MacFarland, Gael Betts

COVER/BOOK DESIGNER: April Mostek

PRODUCTION COORDINATOR: Zinnia Heinzmann

ILLUSTRATORS: Kirstie McCormick, Laura Lee Fritz, Kate Reed, Tim Manibusan, Richard Sheppard

PHOTOGRAPHY COORDINATOR: Rachel Ackley

PHOTOGRAPHY BY Laura Lee Fritz, Sharon Risendorph, Steven Buckley of Photographic Reflections, Bagley Tauber Photography, Luke Mulks, Diane Pedersen

Published by C&T Publishing, Inc., P.O. Box 1456, Lafayette, CA 94549

Library of Congress Control Number: 2025009403

Printed in China

10 9 8 7 6 5 4 3 2 1

DEDICATION

This book is dedicated to all of you whom I have taught in classes across the continent—all of you who taught me to love fabric, to love sewing, to love quilting. It's dedicated to all of you who awakened me to the reality of people actually making my designs. This includes all of you whom I've never even met, and especially those of you whom I have loved through the years.

I get my favorite ideas when I doodle with the needle. Then I trace those to get my patterns

Laura Lee Fritz

Contents

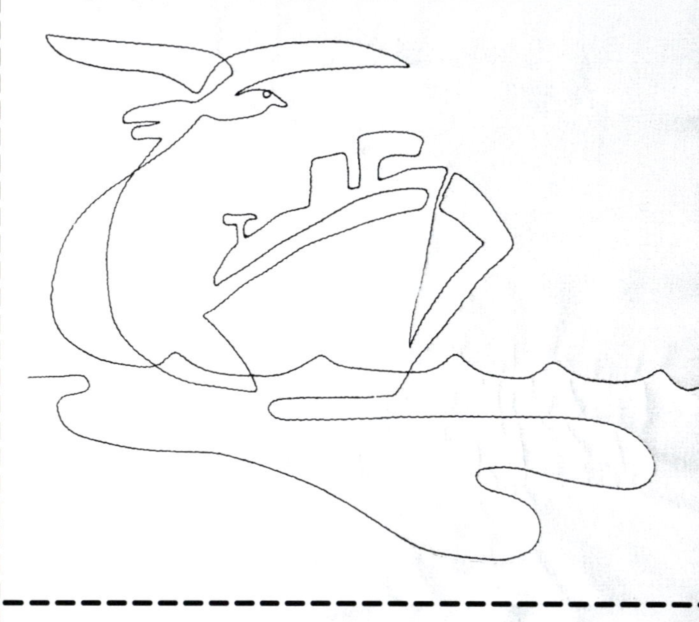

Introduction

When you give a quilt to someone you want them to be crazy-in-love with it. That's what makes the work worth the time. I have some simple tips that can help make sure this happens.

Choose Well. Select a design which excites their passions.

Plan Well. The quilting should not be an afterthought. Can you find plain fabrics to quilt feature designs on? Use them in the patchwork, or for the backing so the design shows up there.

Contrast Well. Contrast thread color helps the feature images stand out against the fabrics. Contrast the direction of the background textures and landscapes against the direction of the lines in the feature images. Contrast the background thread color against the feature thread.

The designs in this book include three categories:

1. Feature images—recognizable and nameable objects and creatures

2. Environments—land, sky, sea, and more

3. Textures—allover and meandering

Combine all three kinds of designs to continue to tell the story of the subject matter in the fabric prints. Stitch an allover design to complement the fabric imagery, or its historical character (a random baptist fan is perfect for a quilt with 1930s-esque fabric; an art deco design would complement a modern quilt).

The bottom line is to ask yourself: *What is the quilt's story, and how can I quilt a design that makes it more wonderful?* There is certainly a design in this book that will make it more wonderful. Have at it.

Using The Designs

Whether you are quilting by hand, on a home sewing machine, or with a long-arm machine, this collection of designs will be a generous resource library. Combine them with each other and with interesting background-filling textures. Enlarge or reduce any of the designs to use on your quilts, and feel free to arrange and combine these ideas with more of your own.

Throughout history quilts have represented people's lives, often expressing a love of story as well as love of color. Many of us don't sit down to conjure up pretty pictures on paper, so we say, *I'm not an artist.*

But being an artist is all in the practice of art. Those of us who make pretty lines attract people who value pretty lines. If we create bold, abstract lines we attract those who value that form. Folk art is a more spontaneous and simple art form. To be an artist, it is sufficient to practice your craft in an expressive way, and follow the path of just *doing it.* You will begin to see the world with a greater attention to what it truly looks and feels like, and those observations will appear in your work.

PLANNING THE DESIGN

If you think of your quilt like a stage and the quilting design as the actors on that stage, designing your overall quilting plan will be easy. One design will act as the lead character on center stage, with a supporting cast of one or more secondary design ideas. Provide some backdrops, such as a background grid and some architecture, and your story will unfold.

Some designs combine interesting shapes but are not made up of recognizable imagery. An overall meandering design is an example of this. Because of their simplicity, these designs don't jump out at you as you study a quilt. You can combine pictorial motifs with allover designs, such as an oak leaf floating in textured waters.

Negative Space

Unquilted areas of a quilt are referred to as negative space. Between your leaves and textures, for example, the blank shapes can be large or small, clumsy shapes or graceful. Be observant of them. A poorly balanced design will have negative space that is confused with the image. Negative space can also be so large that the quilt seems to be underquilted, or so small that the quilting lines are hard to interpret. Try to find balance and clarity in your use of negative space.

Border and Main Designs

If you're planning the background design for borders, consider crossing the border lines into the main design area. This creates a smooth transition between the two areas, and you can work all the side borders as you progress down the quilt. Keep transition and escape routes in mind; they need to be consistent with the shape or feel of the background quilting in order to remain invisible.

Customizing Projects

For a whimsical or a folk-art look, draw or quilt freehand, just looking at the design in front of you.

Create your own whole-block motifs by enlarging an image (or set of images) to fill the block to within an inch of the seams. All the areas within the block that are not filled with the image need to be completed. Could a secondary image be added to fill the blanks? Or an opposing-direction texture be used as fill? What about adding an extension or flourish to the design to complete the block? The goal is to not leave any area unquilted that would loft above the feature design, competing for center stage. Connect all the design areas you add to the main image(s).

To join various designs to make your own borders, find the idea that connects the images: Flowers may connect insects together, leaves connect flowers, a landscape connects horses, or prairie grasses connect pheasants. Be sure to make your drawings of the connecting imagery large enough to fill the negative spaces.

A design can be started from many choices of location: The foot of a horse provides two entry points; its tail provides another entry point. To start a horse image near the face or along its back would be distracting. Try some options and choose the least noticeable one.

Sometimes you will need to slow your needle speed for the short-line designs (an insect) and speed it up again for the long, smooth shapes (a calla lily next to the insect). Practice will show you where you need to pay more attention, and where you need to change your speed to control stitch and shape quality.

TRANSFERRING DESIGNS

If you aren't ready to make the leap into free-motion quilting, there are simple methods to transfer the designs onto your quilt top.

Soluble Stabilizers

There are some great materials to help bring the designs to the cloth for you to stitch. If I am not going to wash the project before parting with it, I use dissolvable films and wash-away *papers*, which I peel off. If I know I am going to launder the entire project before finishing it, I use a wash-away *fabric* (some of which are adhesive). Most wash away fabrics come on rather narrow rolls or pages, but you can find products which are extra wide, for "whole cloth" quilting. I particularly recommend the Solvy line of fabric stabilizers and papers by Sulky.

Paper or Tulle

Trace the designs onto paper with a black permanent pen. Resize as needed. Then, trace the design onto stencil plastic and cut it out. You may prefer to trace the design onto tulle, then draw through the tulle onto the quilt top. Both of these methods are a means to draw directly onto the quilt top with chalk or a fabric pen that is air or water soluble. You may also choose to freehand draw with one of these marking tools.

START QUILTING

Practice "finger drawing" designs before you mark a quilt or start freehand quilting. Tracing your finger over the design two or three times helps to make you more familiar with how the design flows. In turn, when you actually quilt it, your work will be more fluid.

Note any pattern sections where you change sewing direction, sew over an area twice, or sew over an existing line of stitching. You may find it helpful to draw arrows on the pattern to guide you. For most of the patterns, the starting and stopping points are marked. You can start at either end of the pattern and sew left to right or right to left.

When you start or end a line of quilting, or when the top thread or bobbin is depleted, knot the end(s) of the stitching line and thread a needle with the thread tails. Use a long-eye sharp embroidery needle for the tail so both threads will fit through at once. Wrap the pair of threads around the eye tightly, pinch the thread to hold the tiny loops as you withdraw the needle, then slip the eye over these tight little loops. Sew these ends by sliding the needle back along the quilting line, pulling the needle out, and burying the knot into the batting before cutting the tail.

350 MEANDERING & ALLOVER DESIGNS

Meandering Designs

AN INTRODUCTION TO MEANDERING

The word *meandering* has become a catchall for any scribble pattern done all over a quilt. In truth, this word has individual definition beyond the vague use it often gets. Meandering came into use by machine quilters who needed a word to describe a type of design that wandered all over a quilt without crossing other lines without having any other definable form. So it's an *apparently* random sort of pattern. But note my use of the word *apparently*—in order to appear random, a good design has to have a set of rules.

My jigsaw meandering looks like I'm quilting around a quilt covered with coins. I put into mind whether they are dime-sized or quarter-sized, so I can keep the size consistent from start to finish on the quilt.

Jigsaw Meandering

In Italian, the word for worm is *vermicelli.* Vermicelli meandering lines (named for the entertaining earthworm) are much longer.

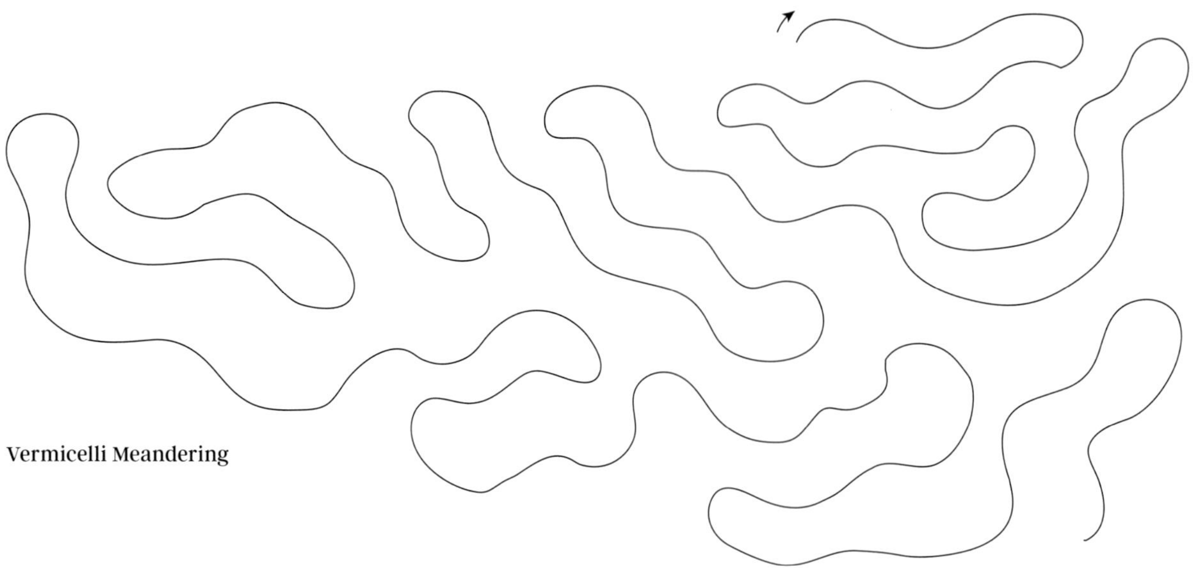

Vermicelli Meandering

Right-angle meandering is mostly square angles.

Right-Angle Meandering

All-points meandering makes use of non-right angles.

All-Points Meandering

My signature meandering combines all four of those styles: jigsaw, vermicelli, right-angle, and all-points.

Laura Lee's Meandering

MEANDERING DESIGNS

What follows is a collection of doodles that meander about within a set of rules unique to each design. More studied design will even require crossing over lines, breaking the classic meandering rules. As a designer, you can make rules just to break them!

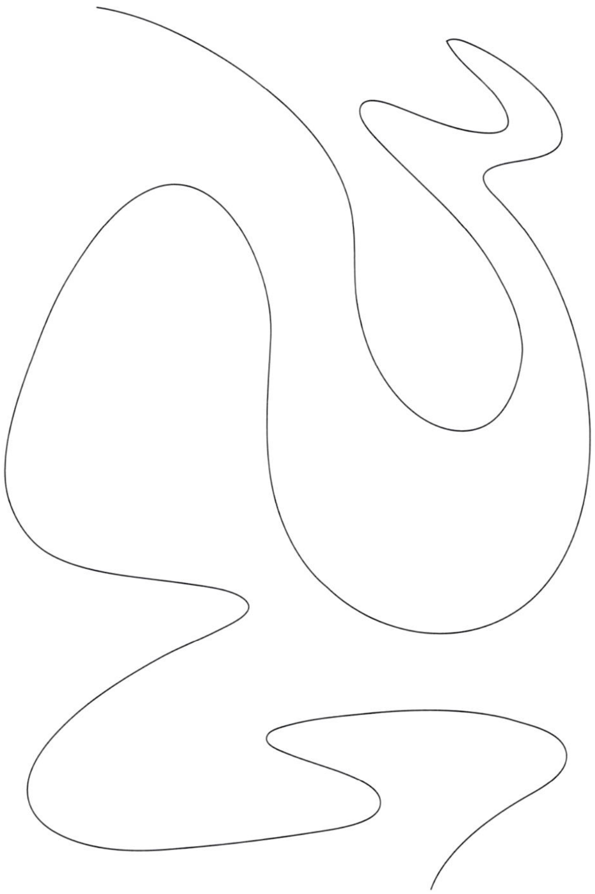

MEANDERING DESIGNS

The dog's eyes are created with a backstitch.

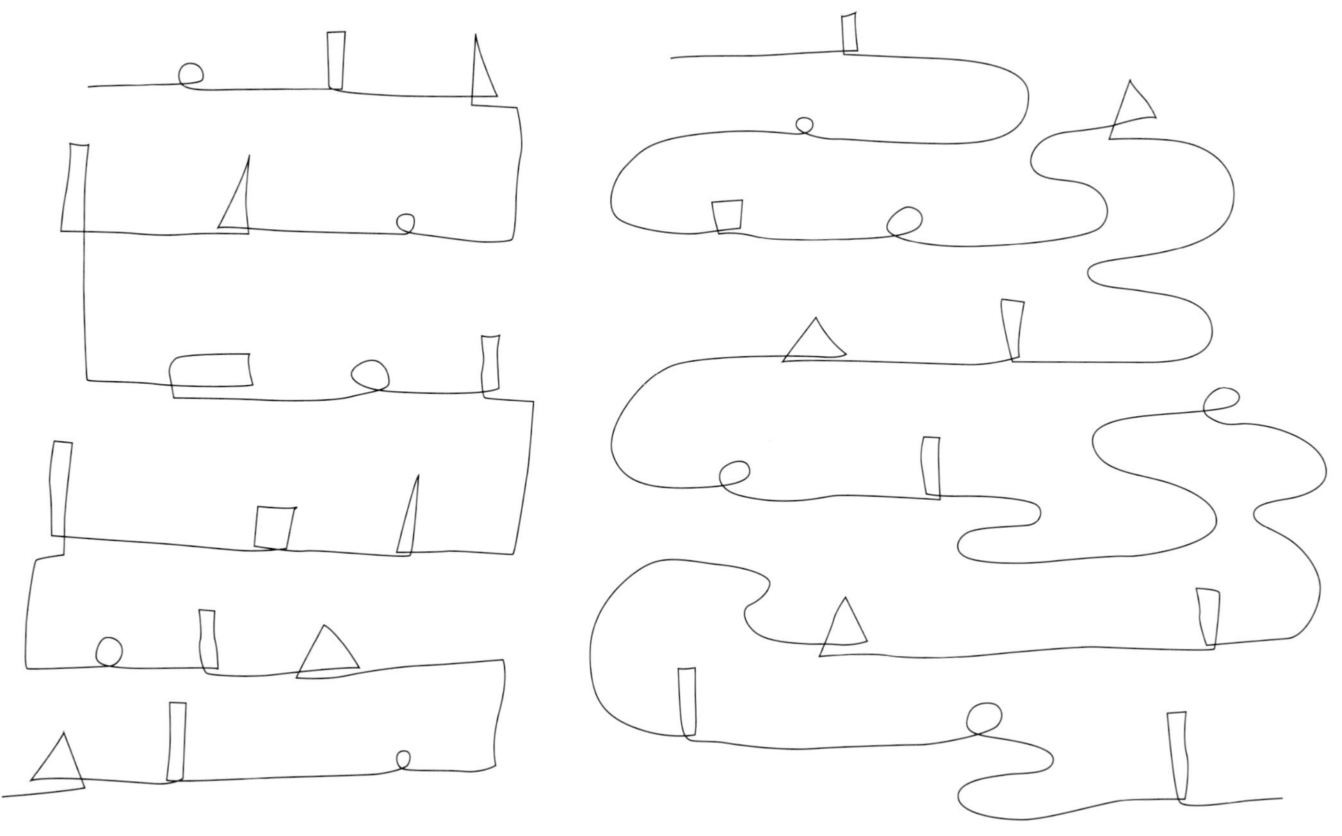

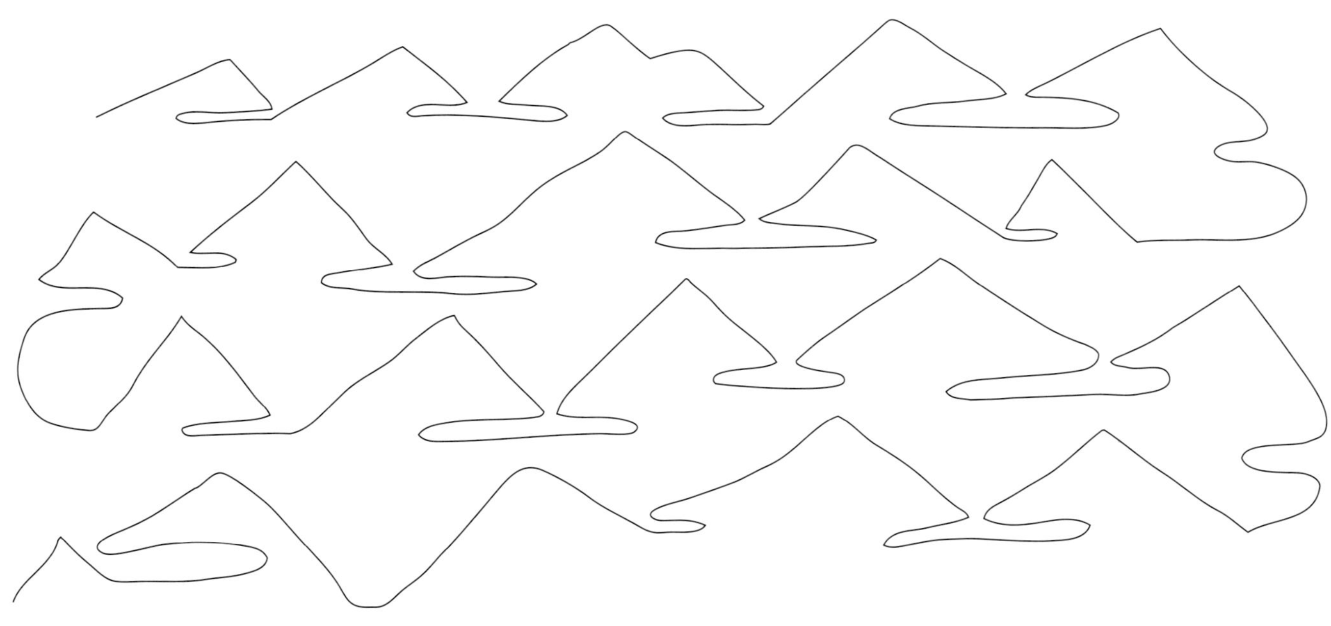

MEANDERING DESIGNS

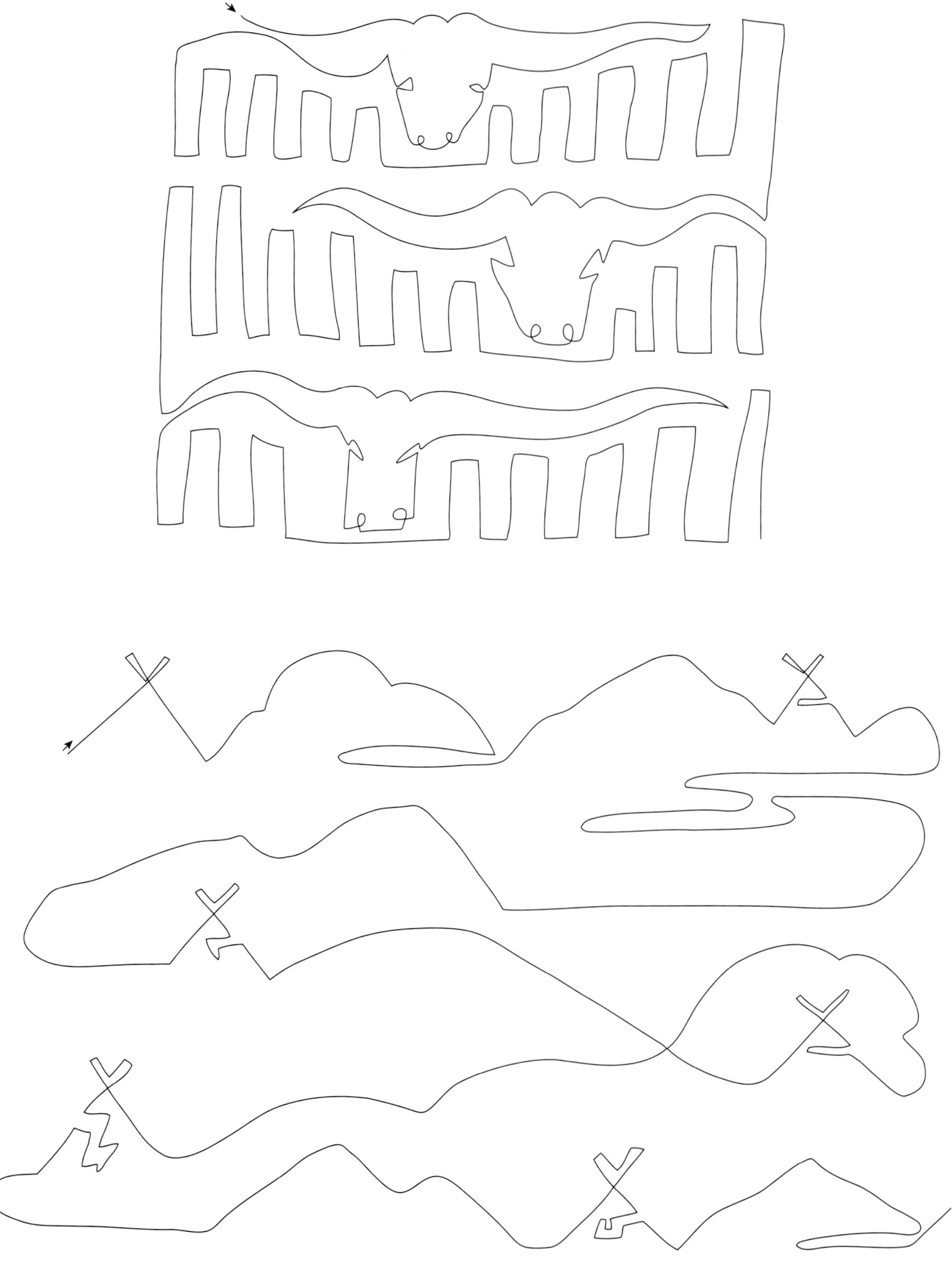

MEANDERING DESIGNS

Square Dancing Designs

AN INTRODUCTION TO SQUARE DANCING

When you are machine quilting a pattern, you begin to feel and hear the beat of the pattern, like music. The beat moves your body like a dance partner. When you goof in the pattern, you can tell by a sense of having missed a beat.

Some quilts, like nine-patches, are made of small pieced squares of the same size. These are perfect for square dancing designs. Use the seam lines to guide your design, and I've designed the quilting patterns to play with the grid format. These square dancing designs are drawn on a layout of dots. The dots represent seams to help you see how the quilting patterns are made in a relationship to the quilt squares. If it helps, take a light-colored pencil and faintly draw in the lines to connect the dots. Enjoy combining more than one grid design in a quilt.

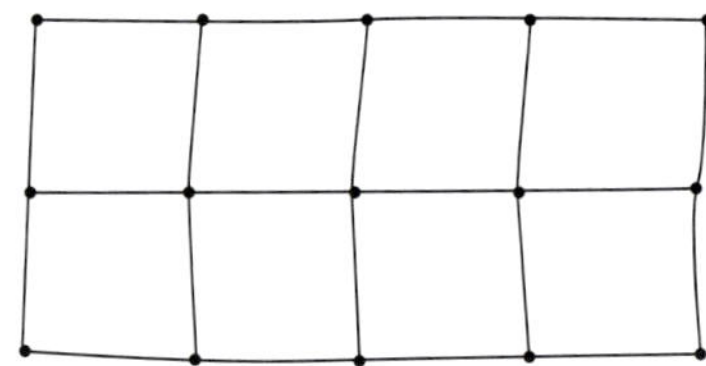

Square dancing grid

SQUARE DANCING DESIGNS

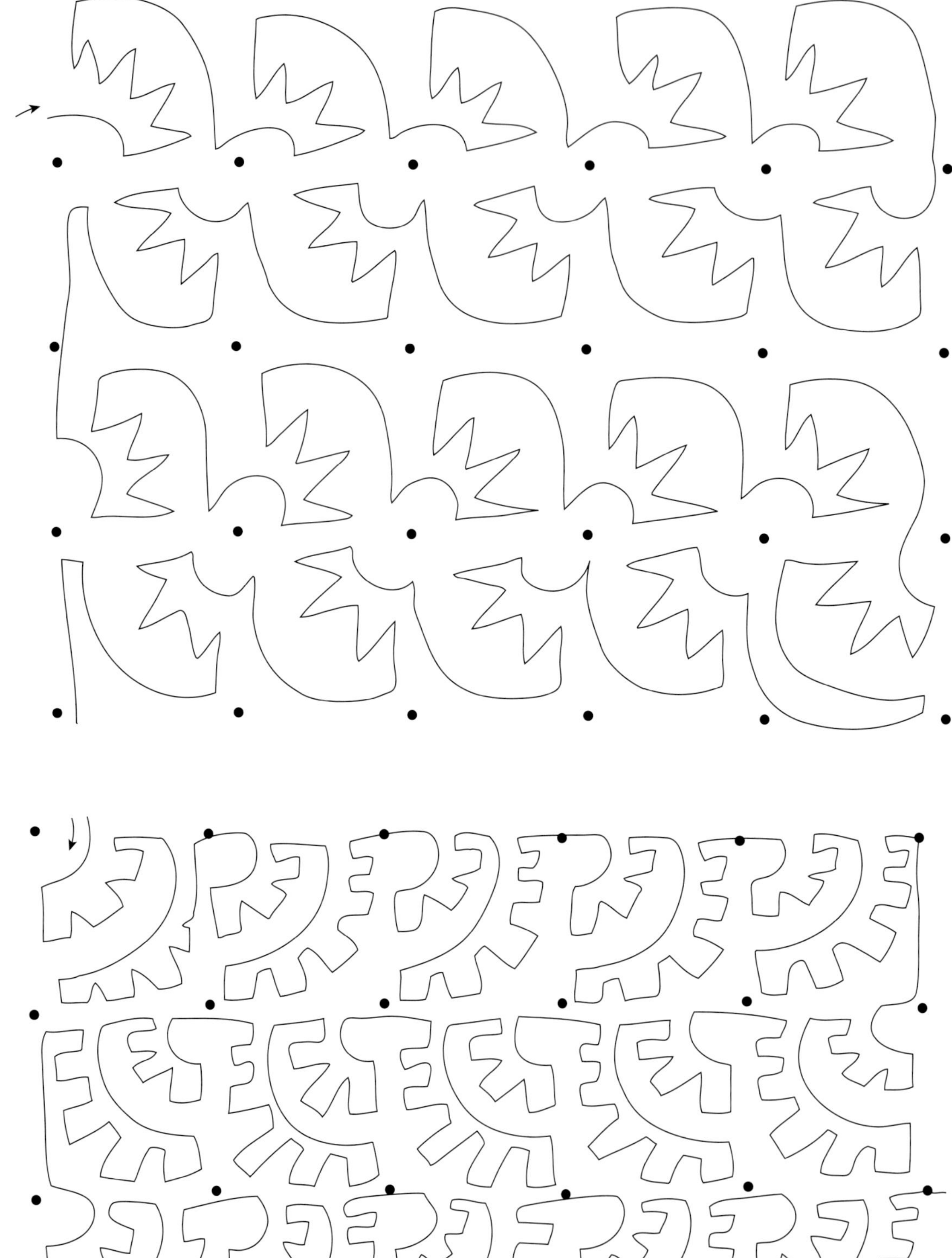

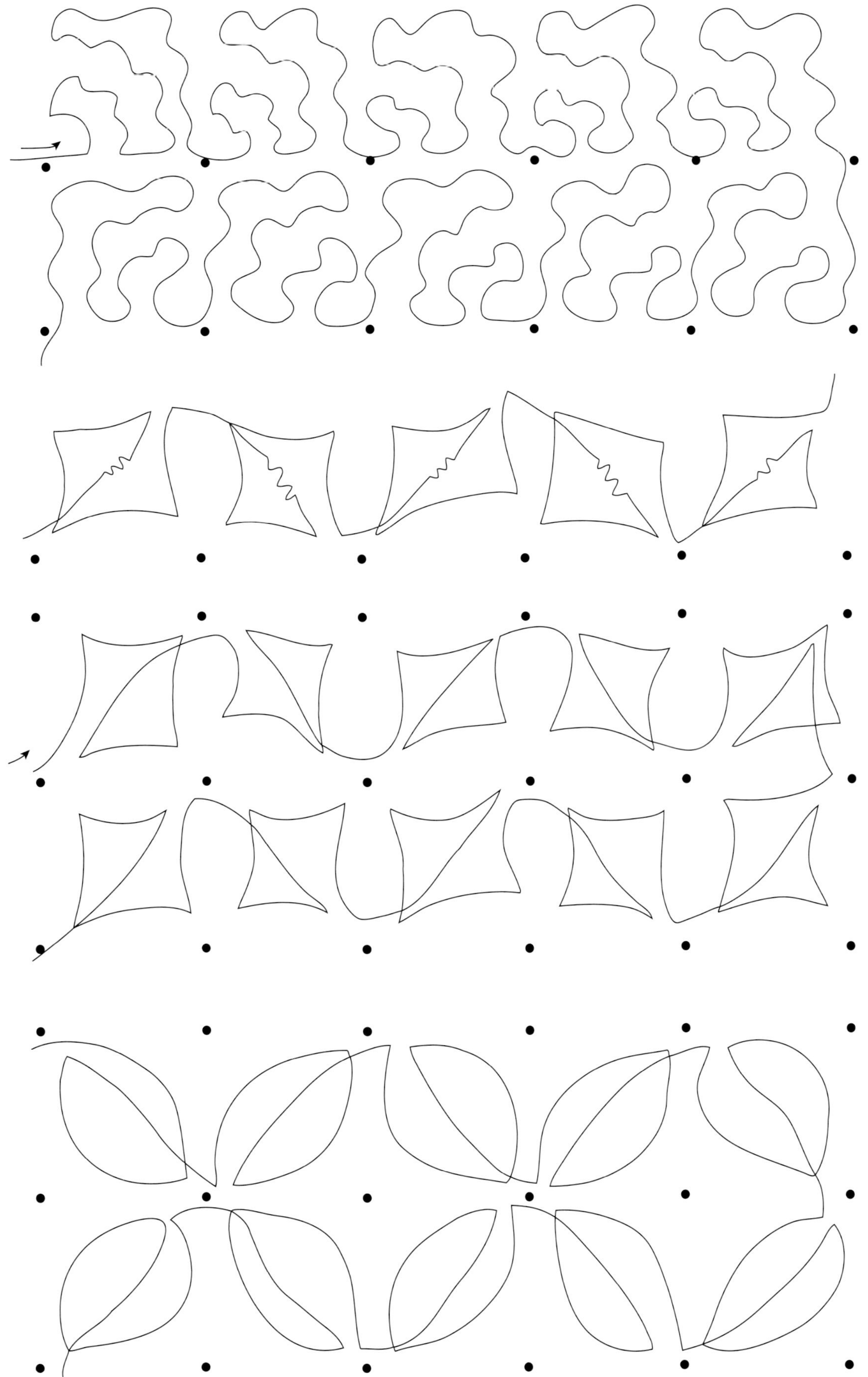

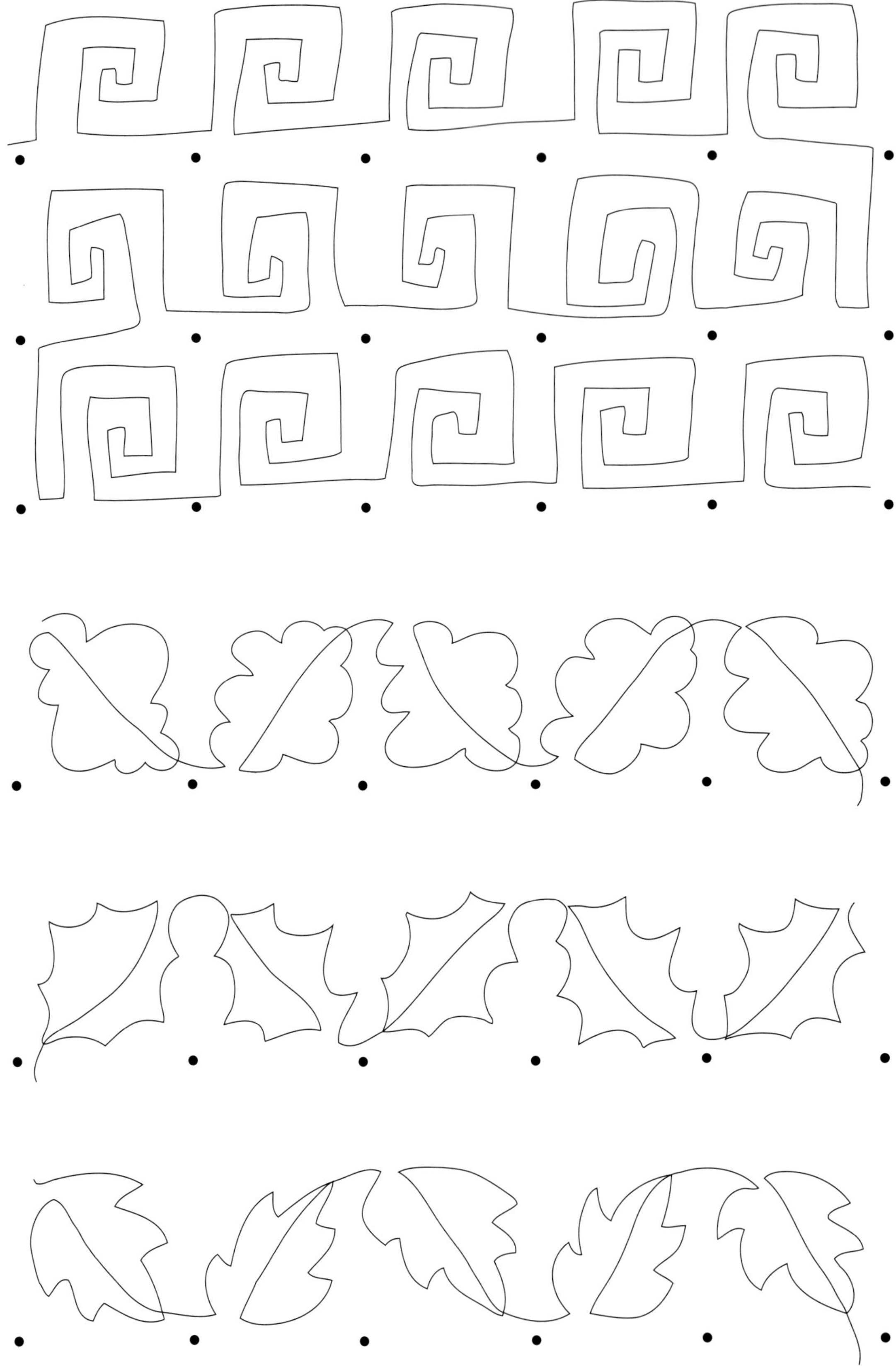

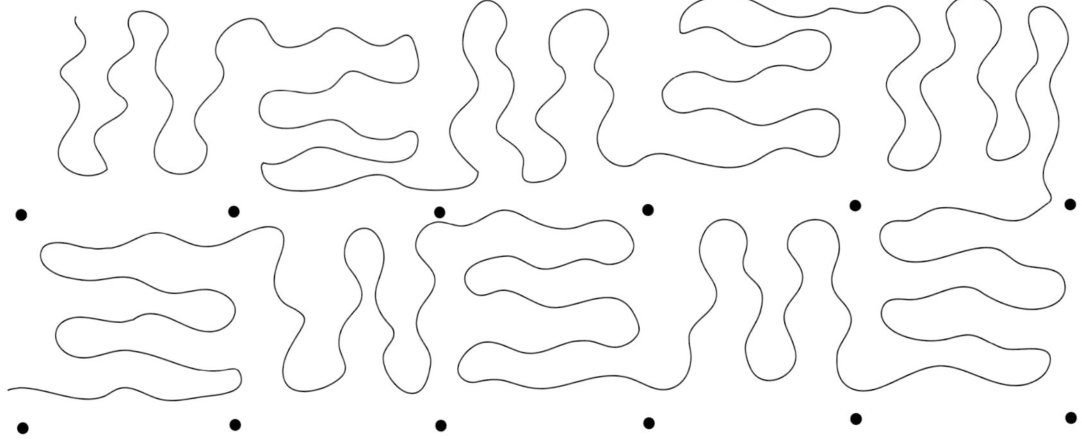

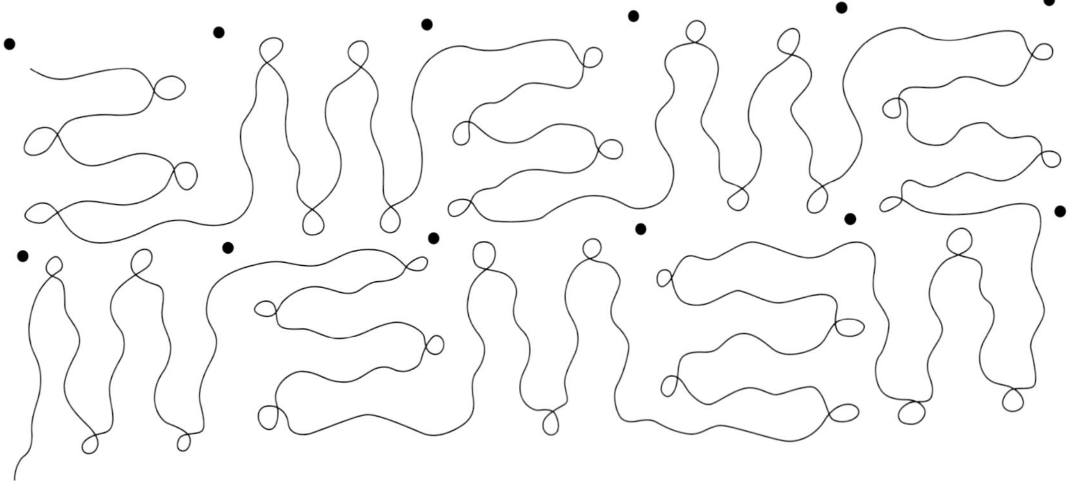

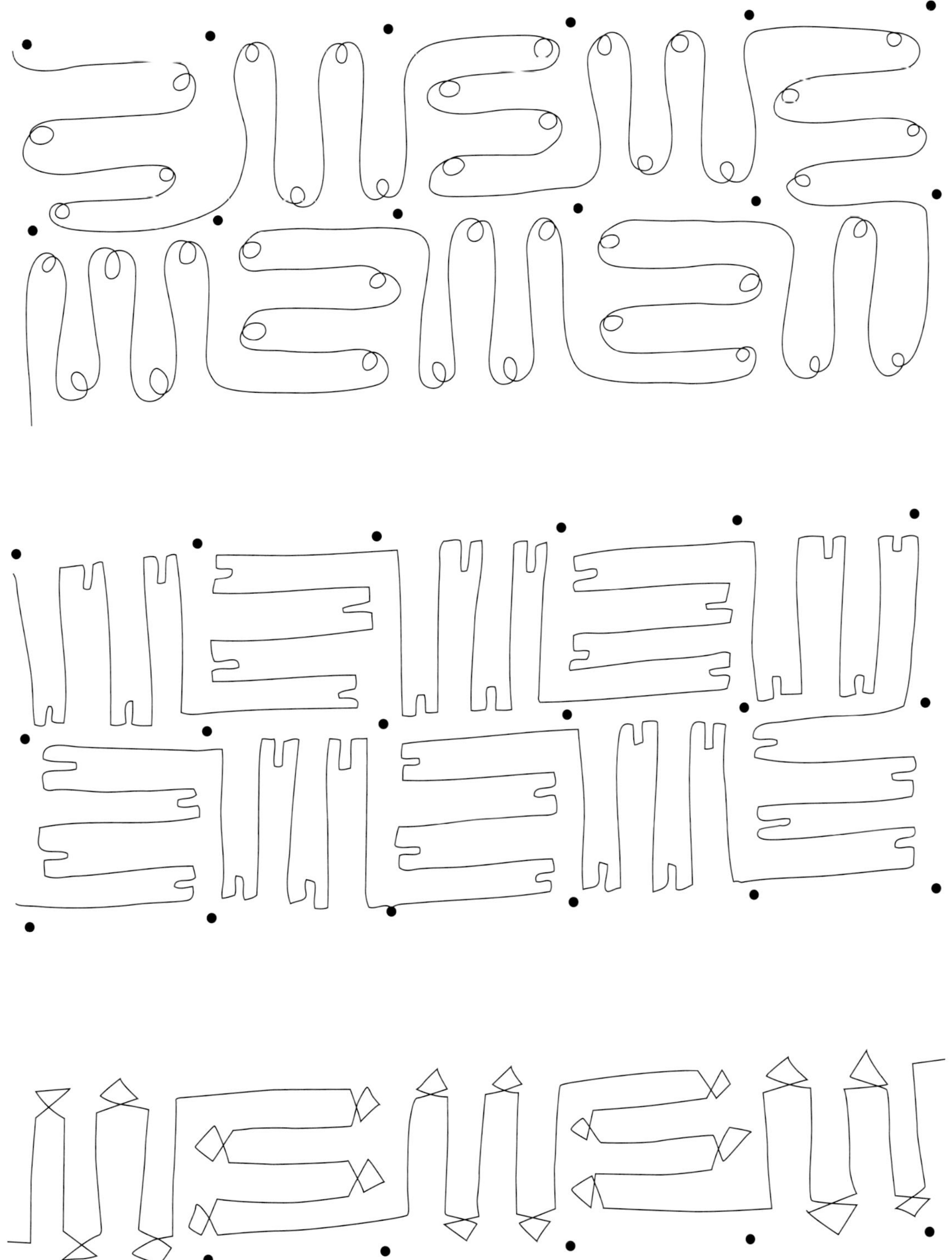

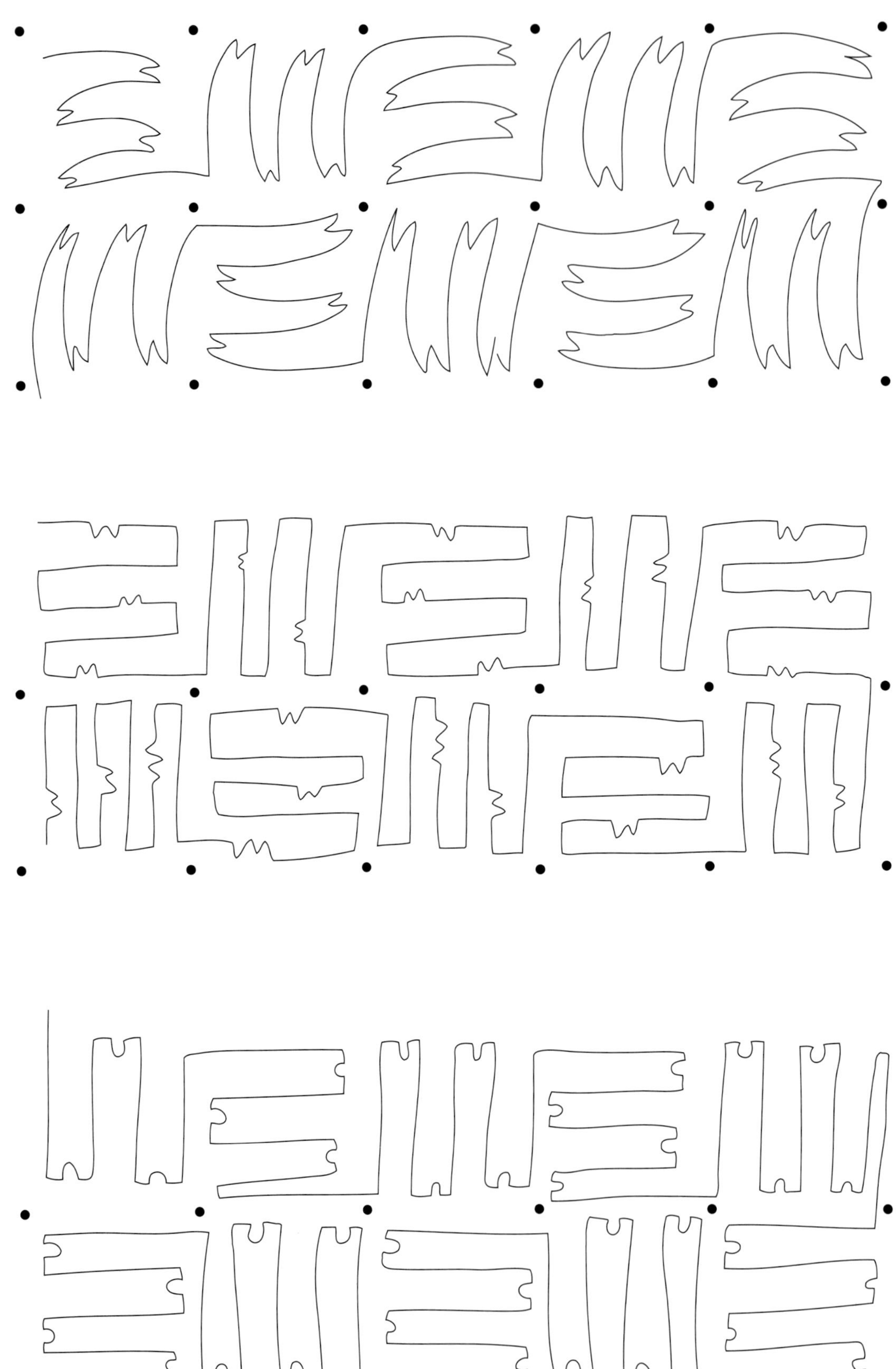

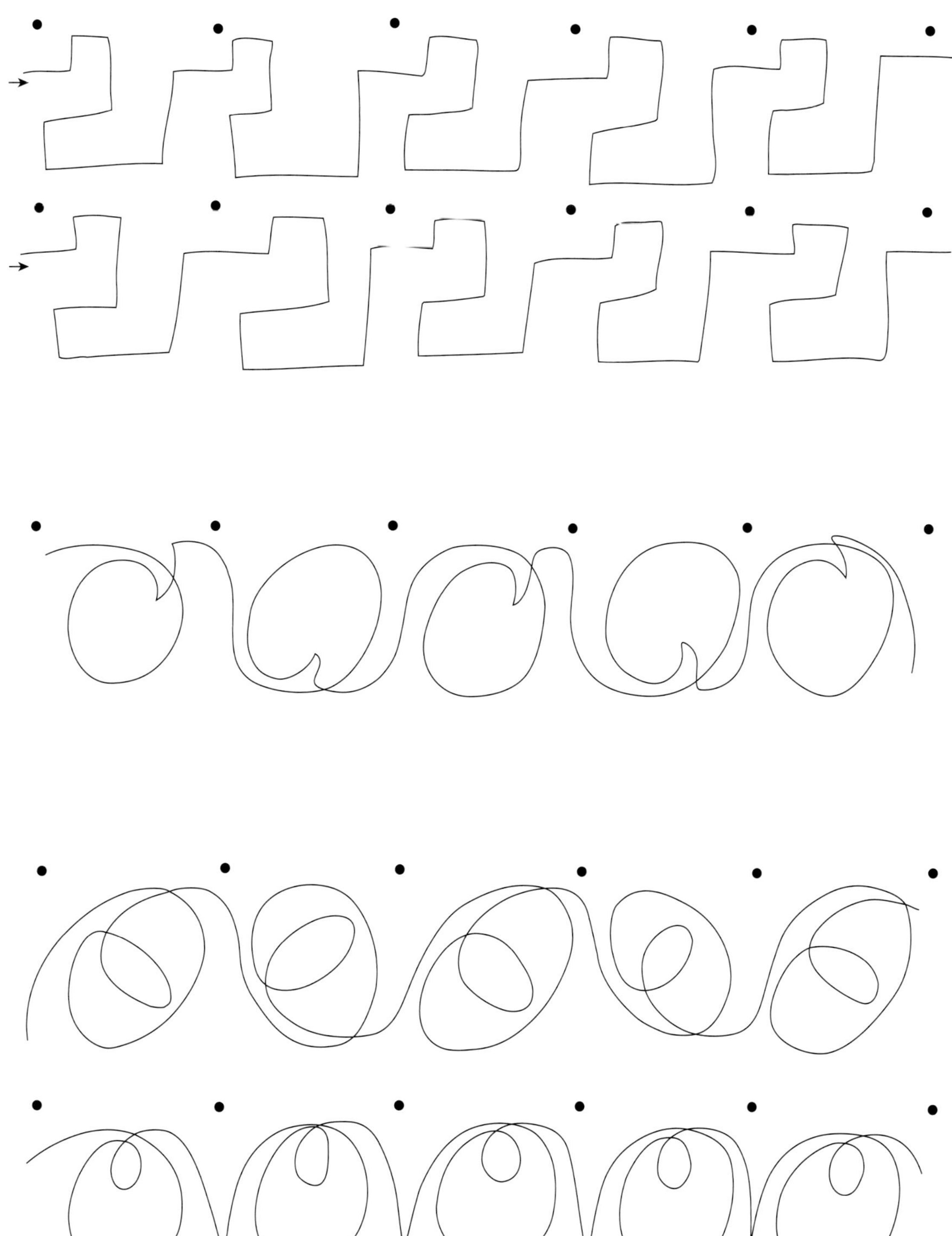

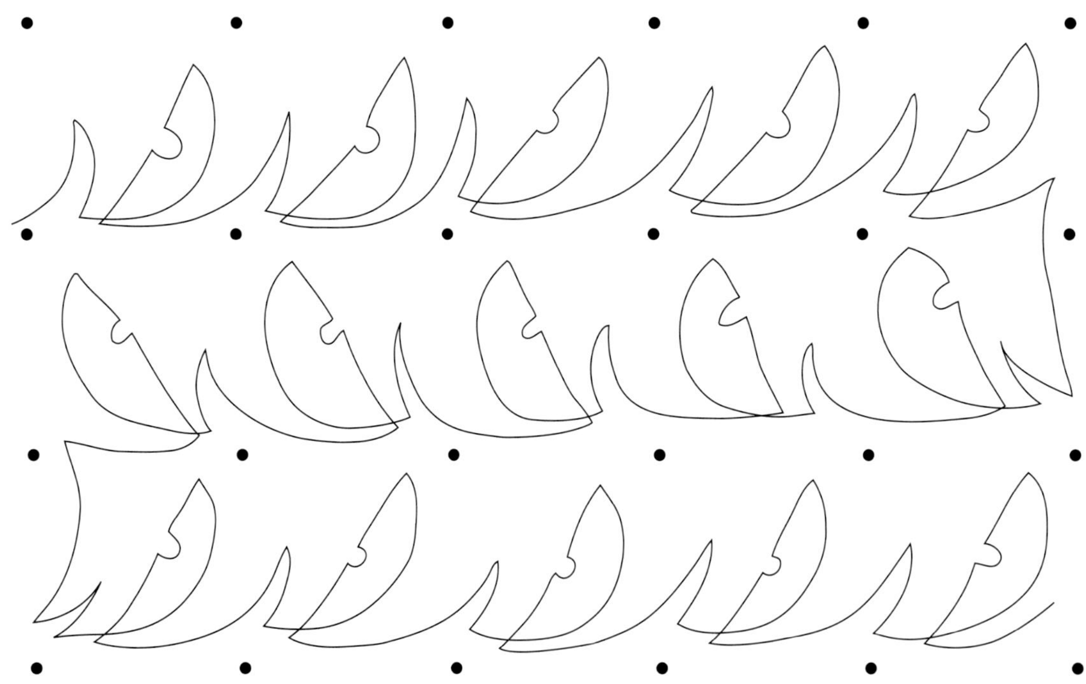

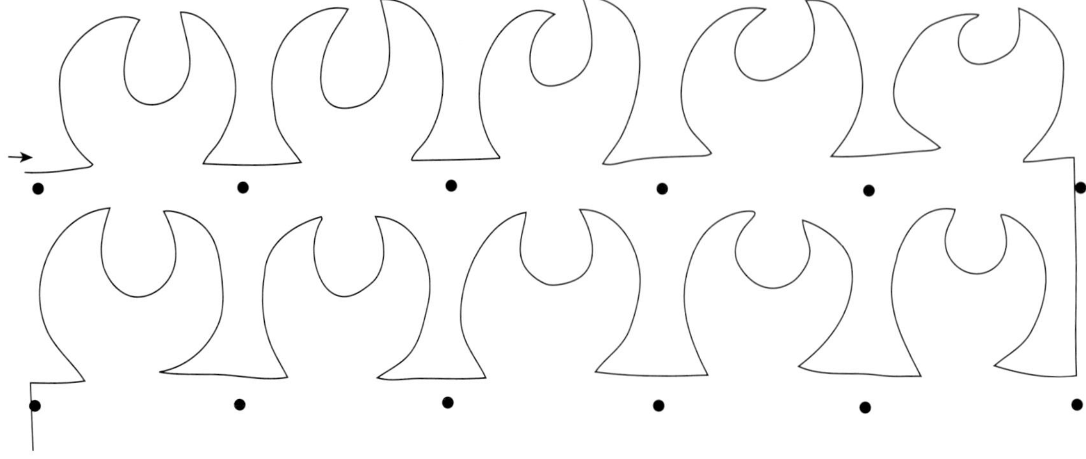

Orange Peel Designs

AN INTRODUCTION TO ORANGE PEELS

The standard quilt block called *Orange Peel* also makes a terrific pattern for quilting a grid of square blocks. When done carefully, you will get the illusion of interlocking rings, similar to a double wedding ring. So many variations are possible that I can call the Orange Peel a format for design, not just a pattern.

To make an Orange Peel design:

- Start in the lower left.
- Draw the same line around 3 sides of the 'square'.
- Continue on to the next 'square'.
- Finish the bottom of the design as you start the next row.

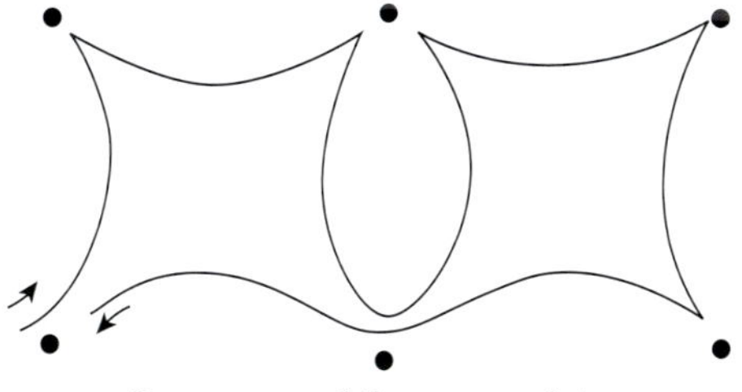

Dance around the seam points

ORANGE PEEL DESIGNS

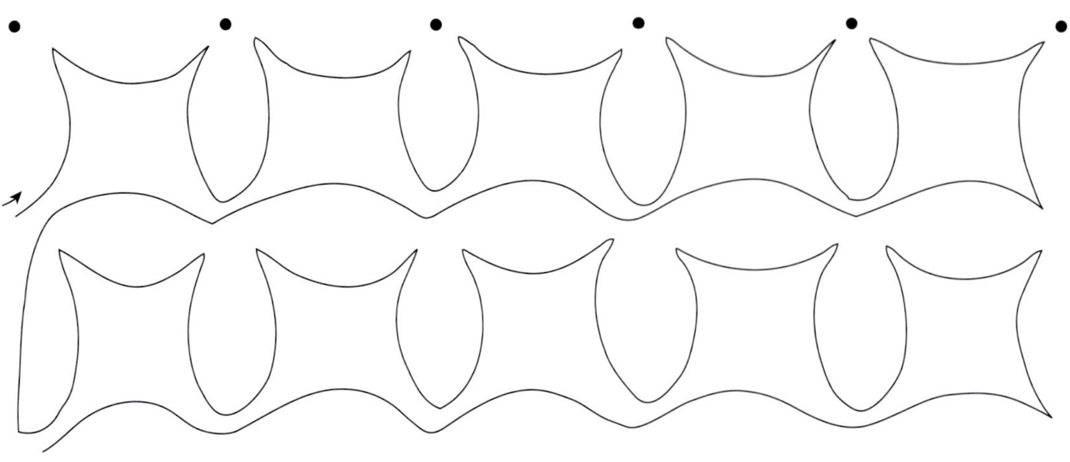

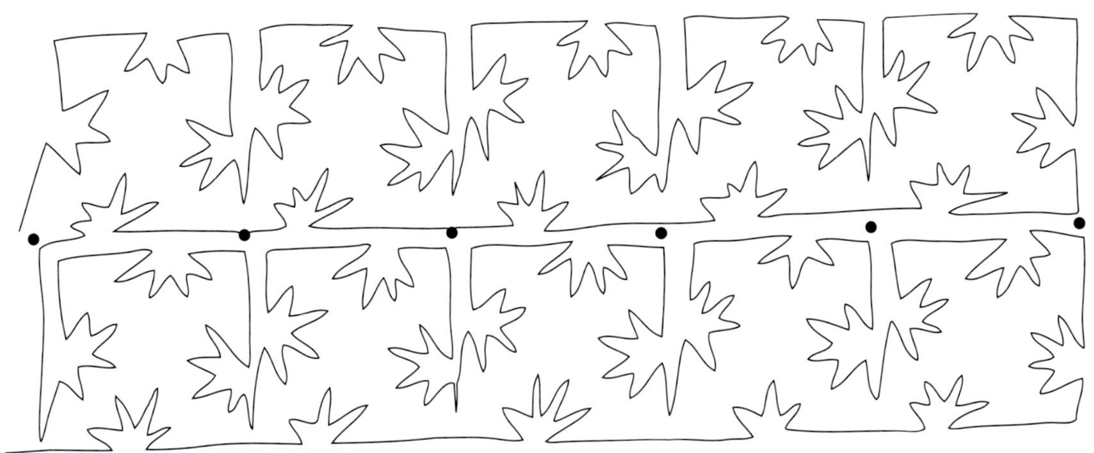

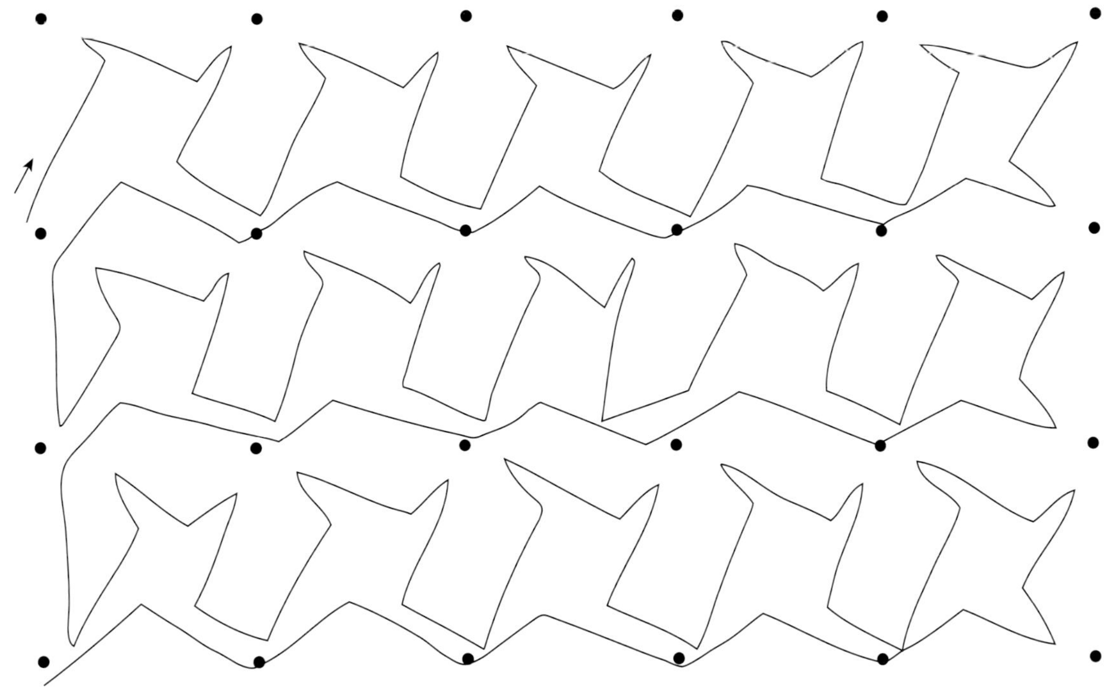

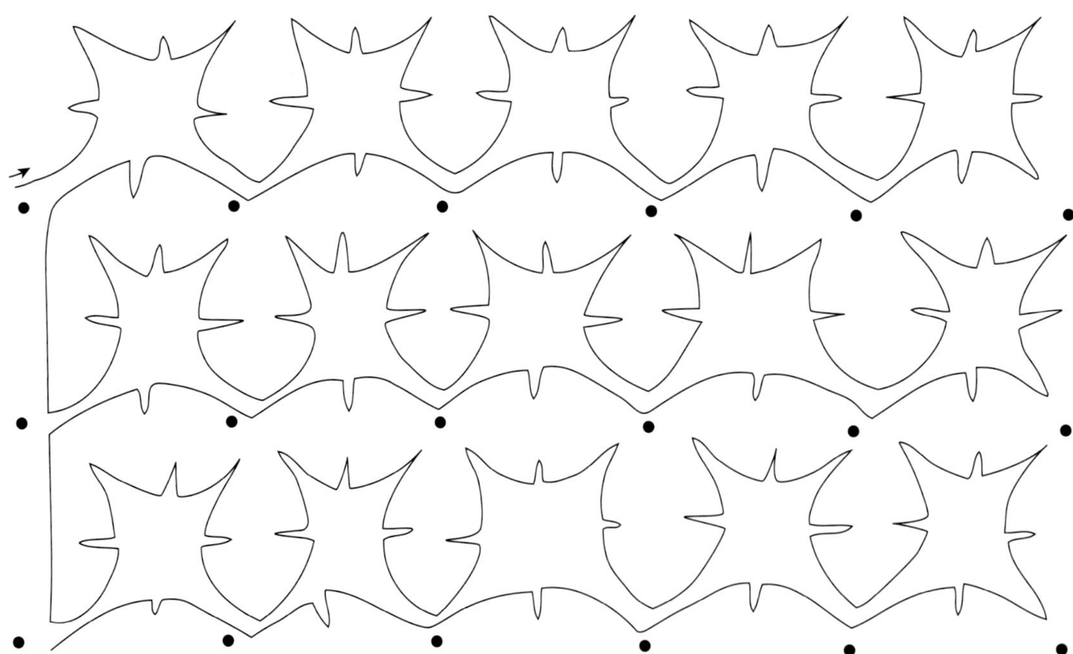

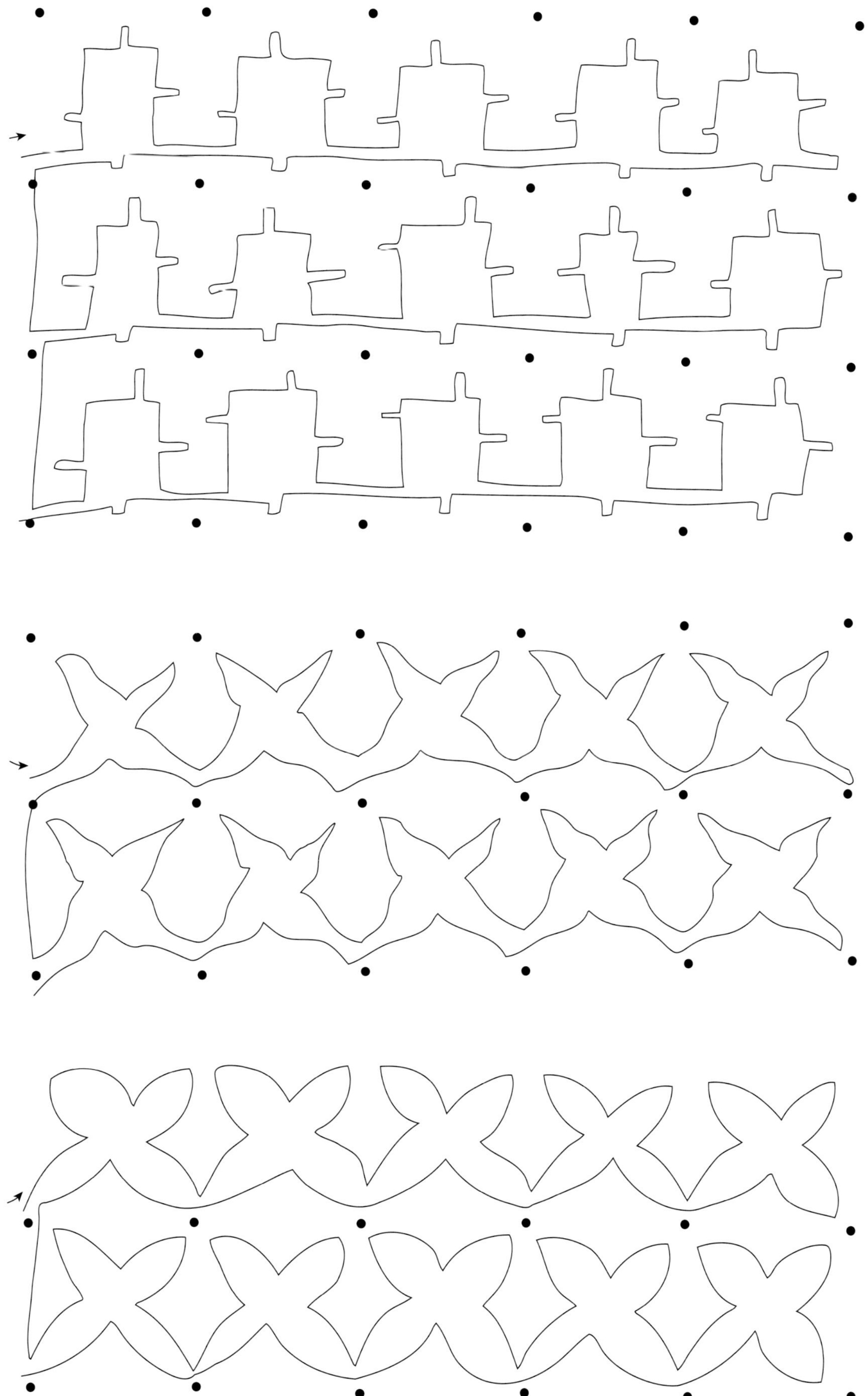

Clamshell Designs

AN INTRODUCTION TO CLAMSHELLS

We know clamshells as a quilting pattern, but let's take a look at its possibilities as a format—a plan for the organization and arrangement of a quilting design. Start with a row of round hills, build a second row staggering—or offsetting—the row of hills. This is the classic clamshell.

Classic clamshell drawn top row first

Classic clamshell drawn bottom row first

Let's define the format. In a clamshell, low points of one row "kiss" the highpoints of the next and previous row. Apply that format to a thundercloud concept, or to a simple V-shape.

Thundercloud clamshells

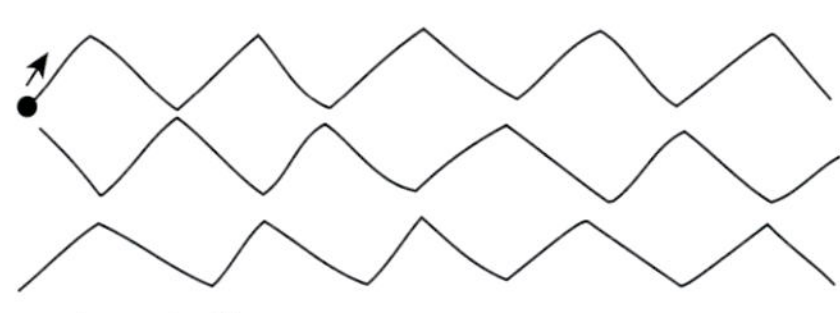

V clamshells

Now you've got some ideas...

CLAMSHELL DESIGNS

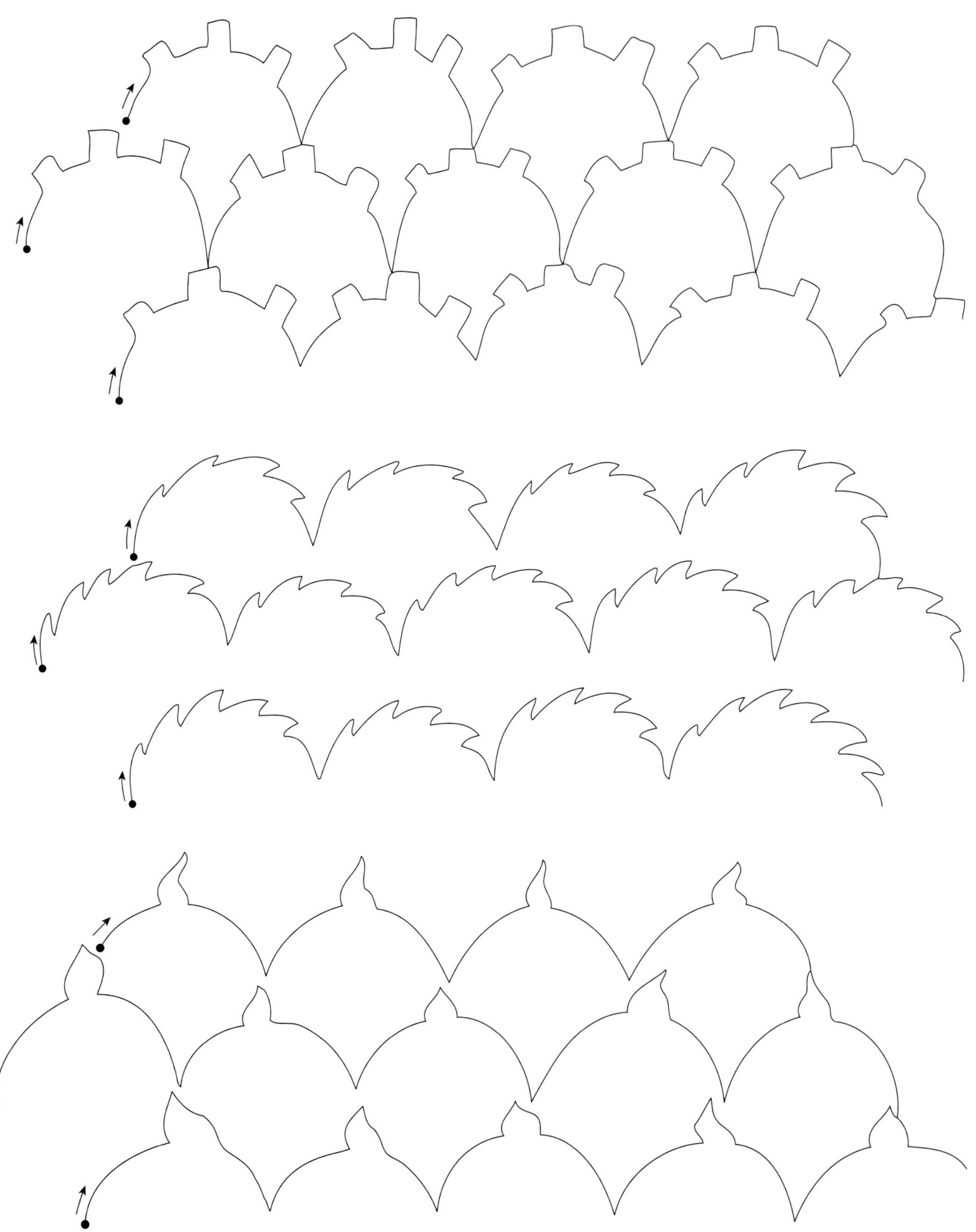

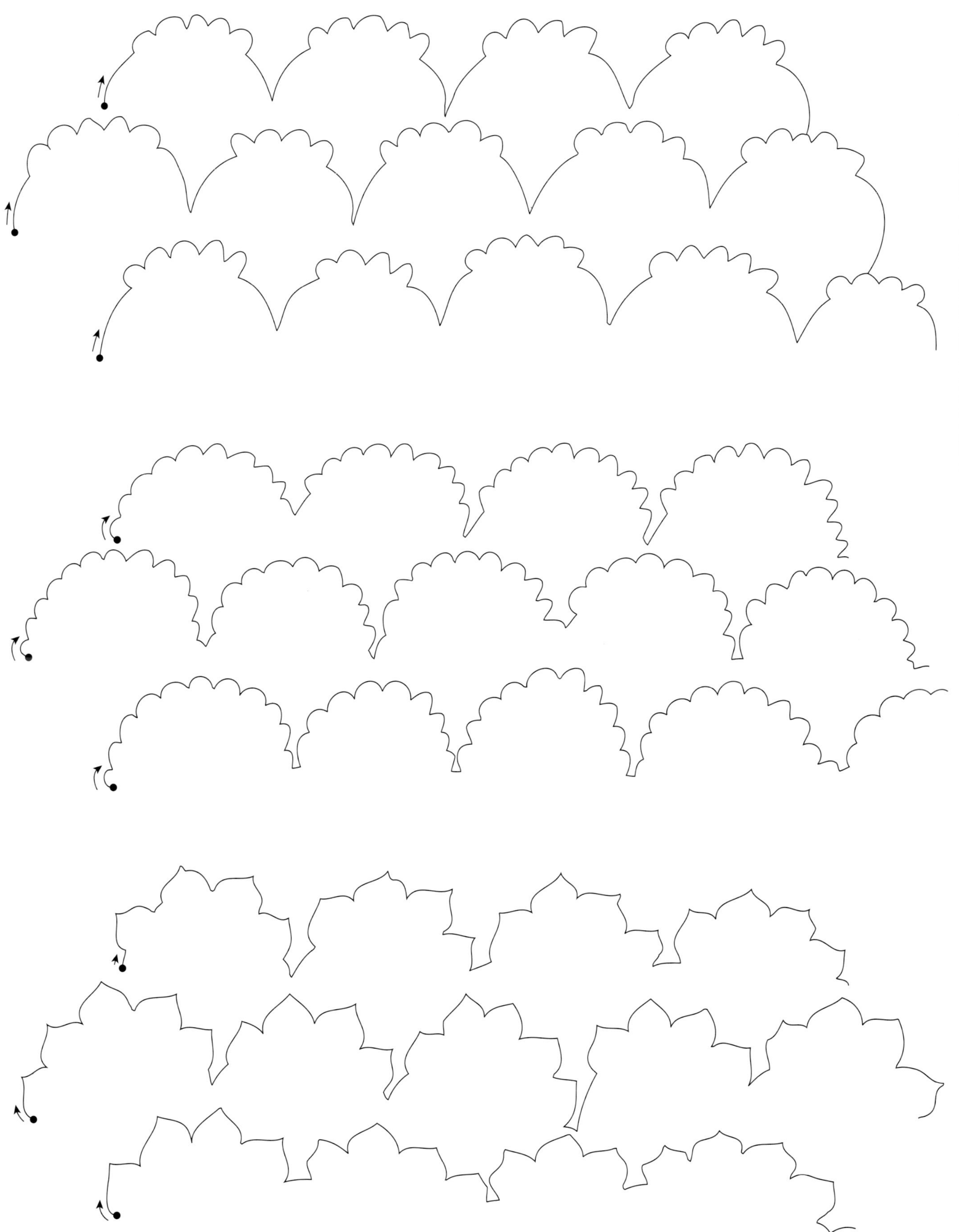

CLAMSHELL DESIGNS

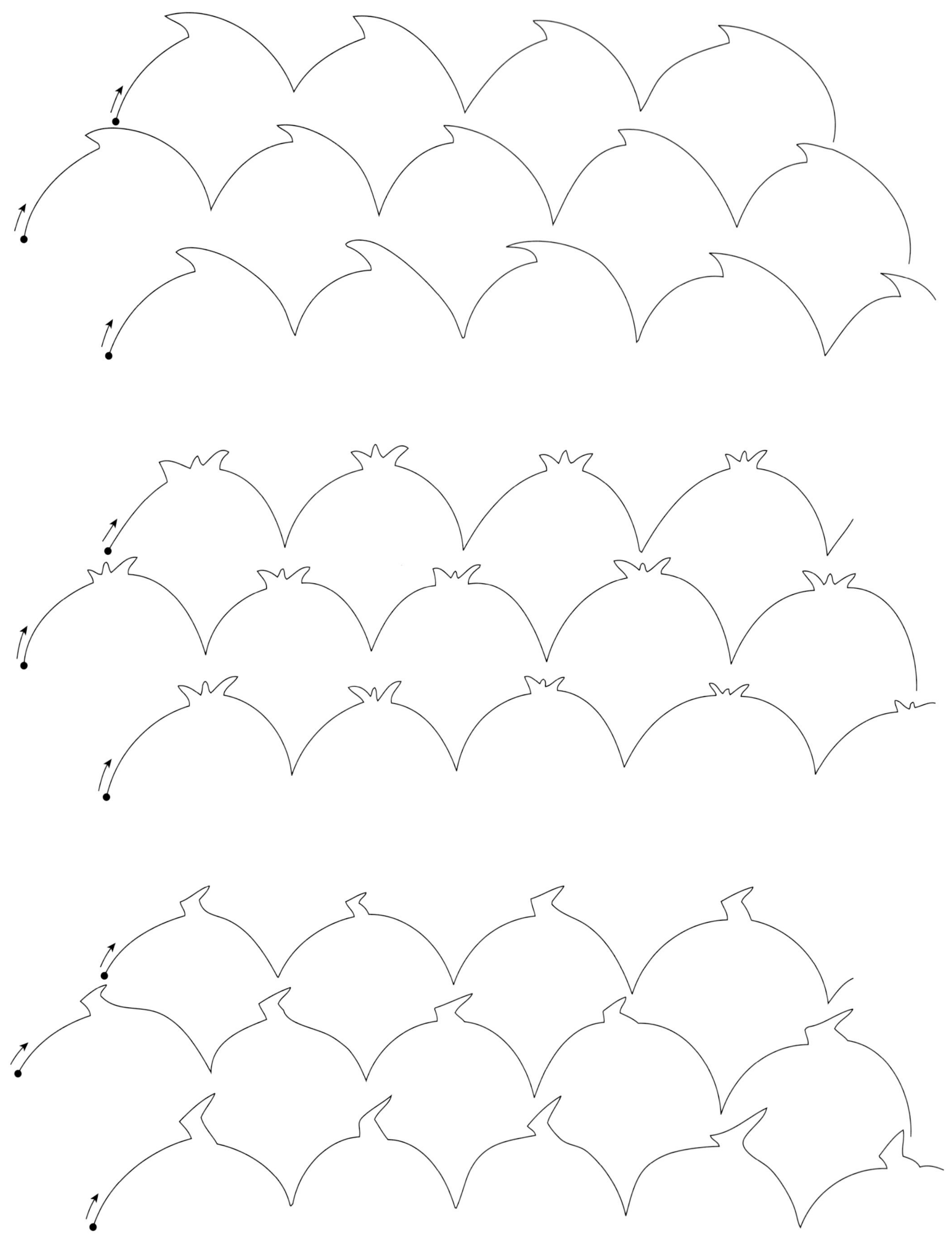

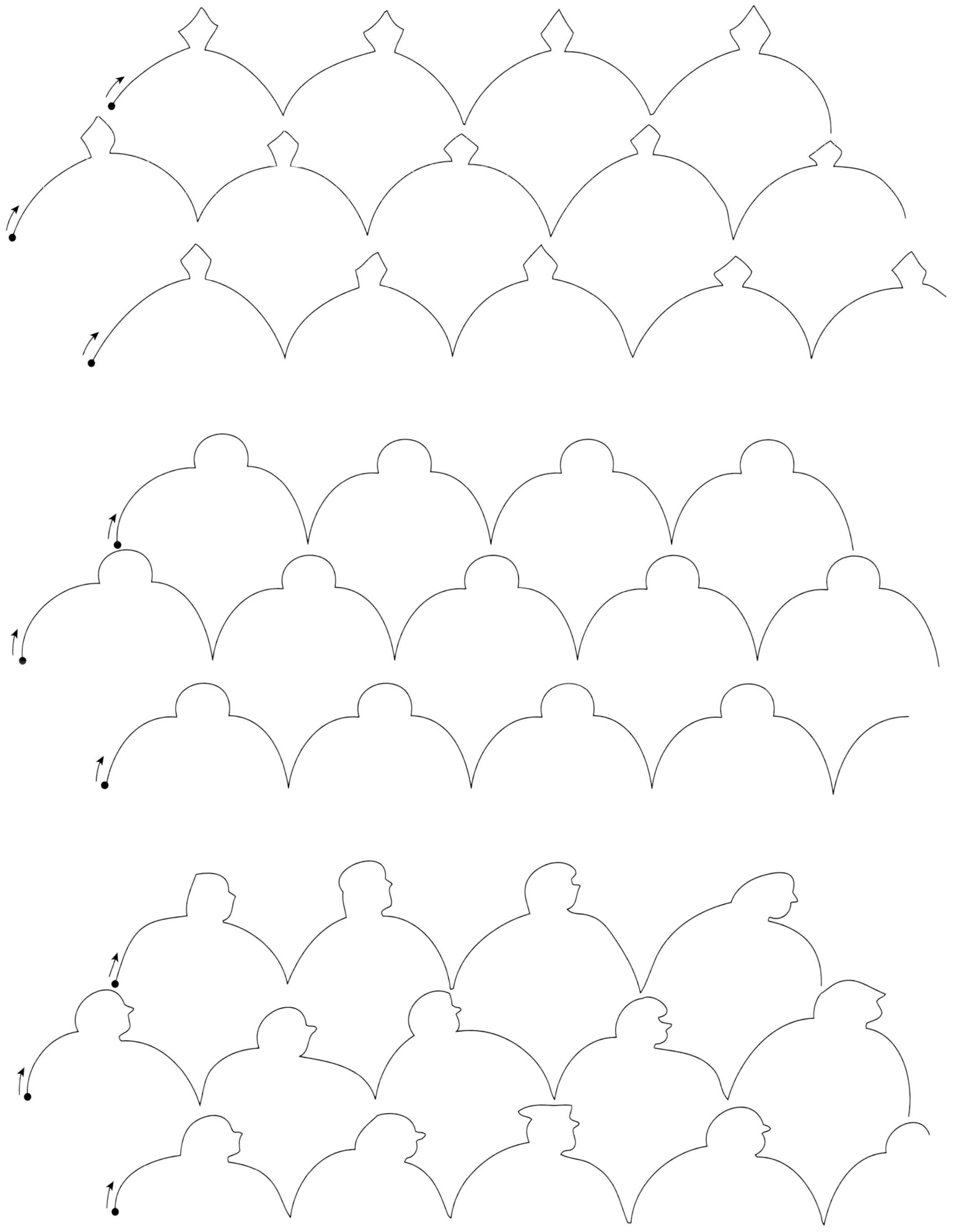

CLAMSHELL DESIGNS

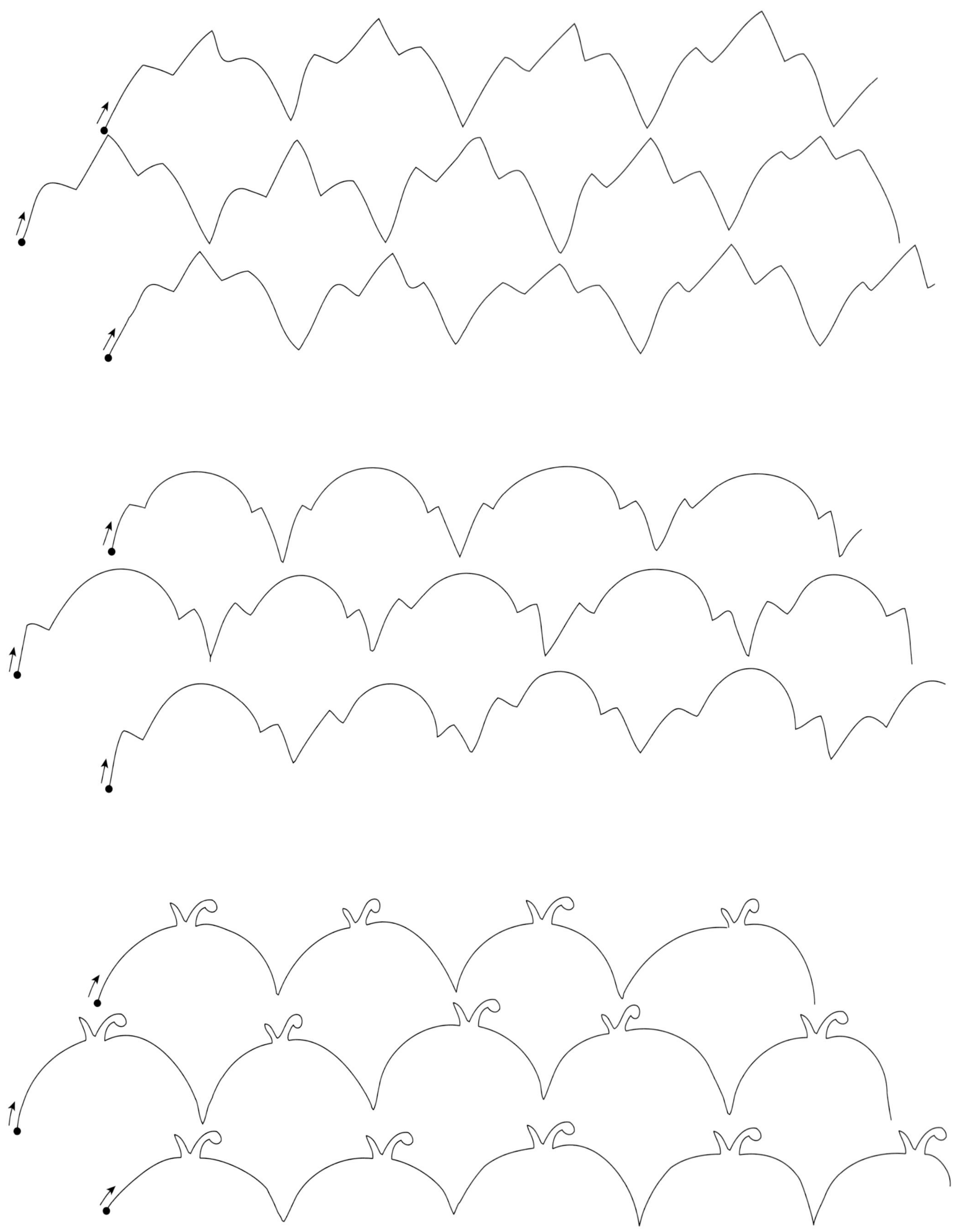

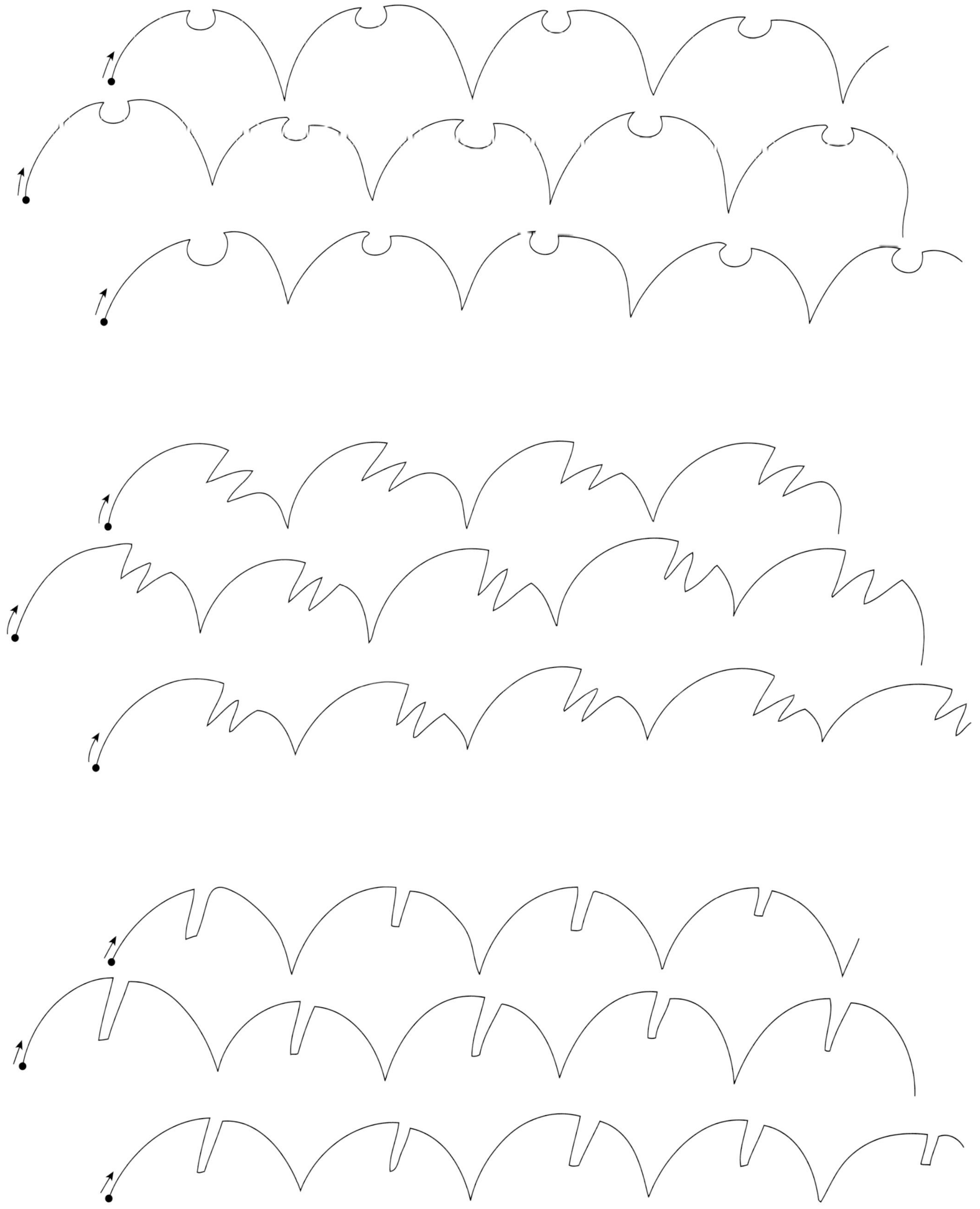

CLAMSHELL DESIGNS

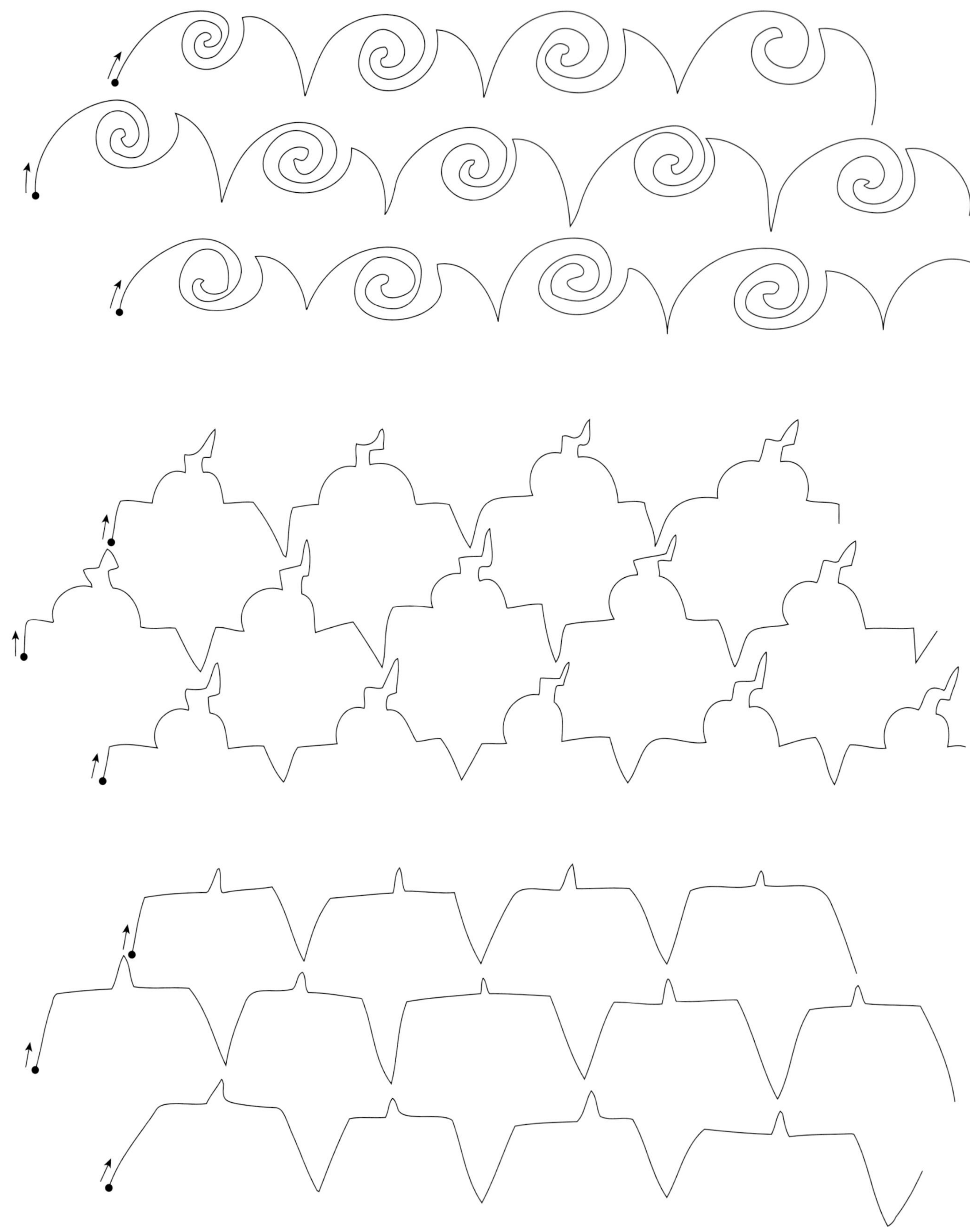

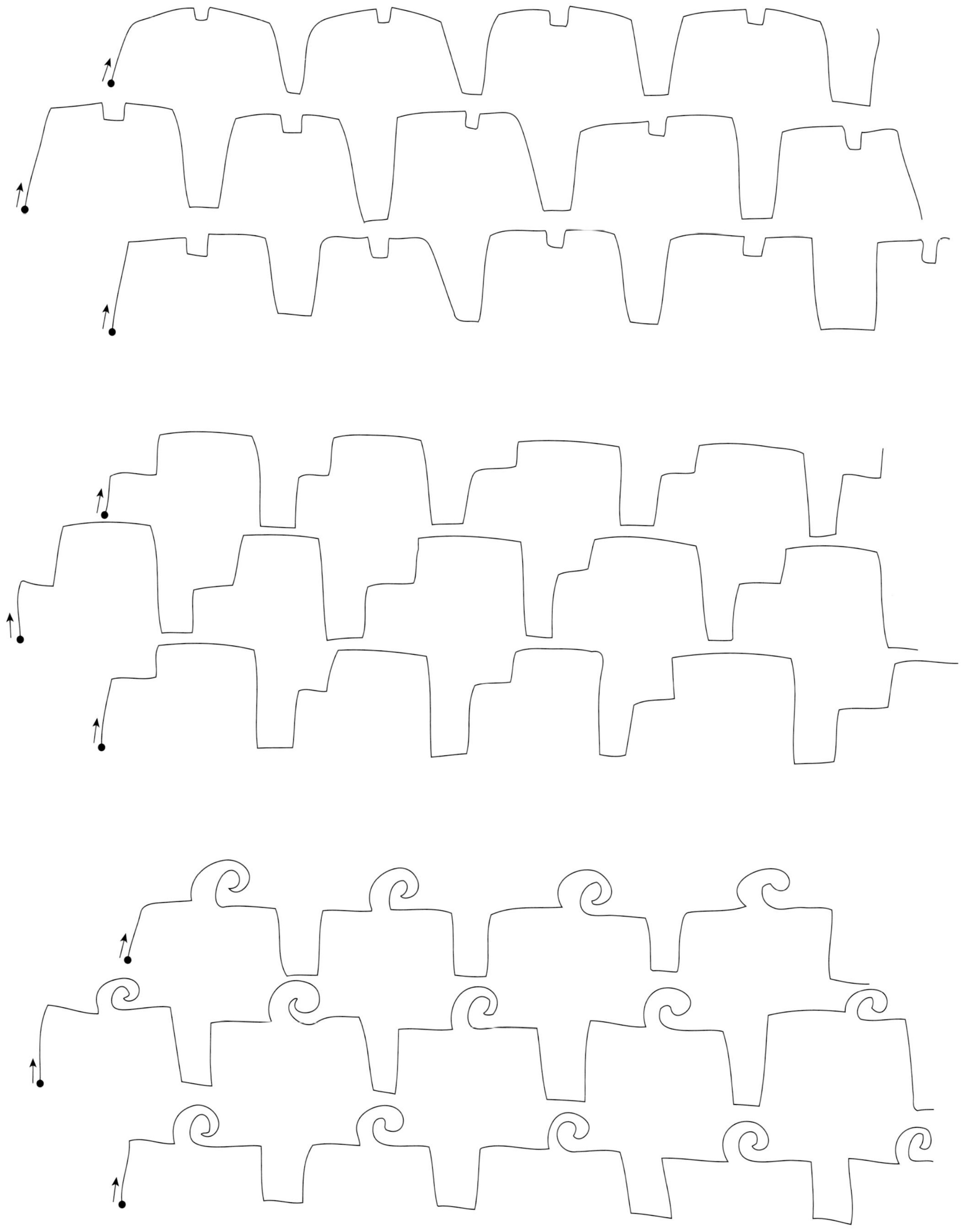

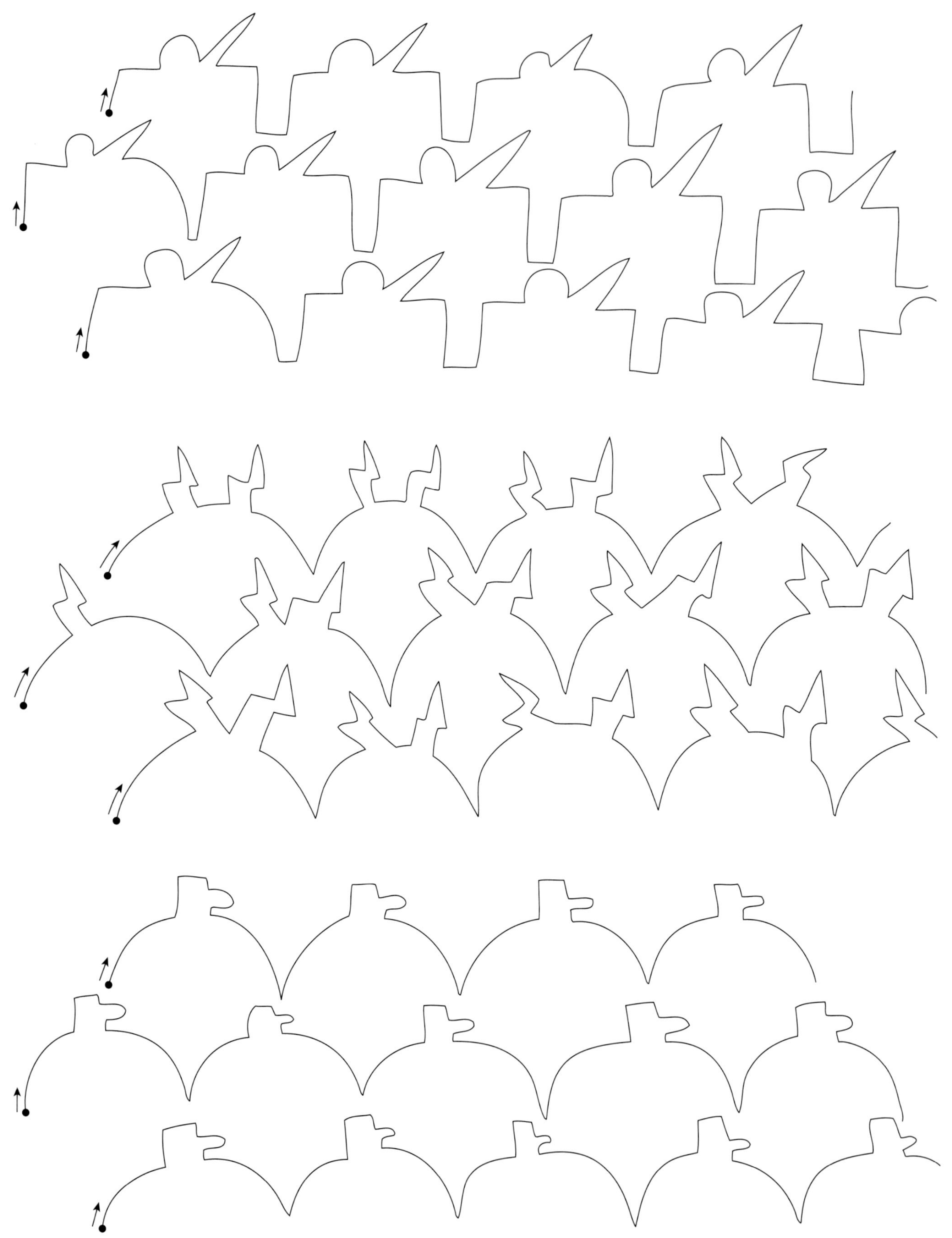

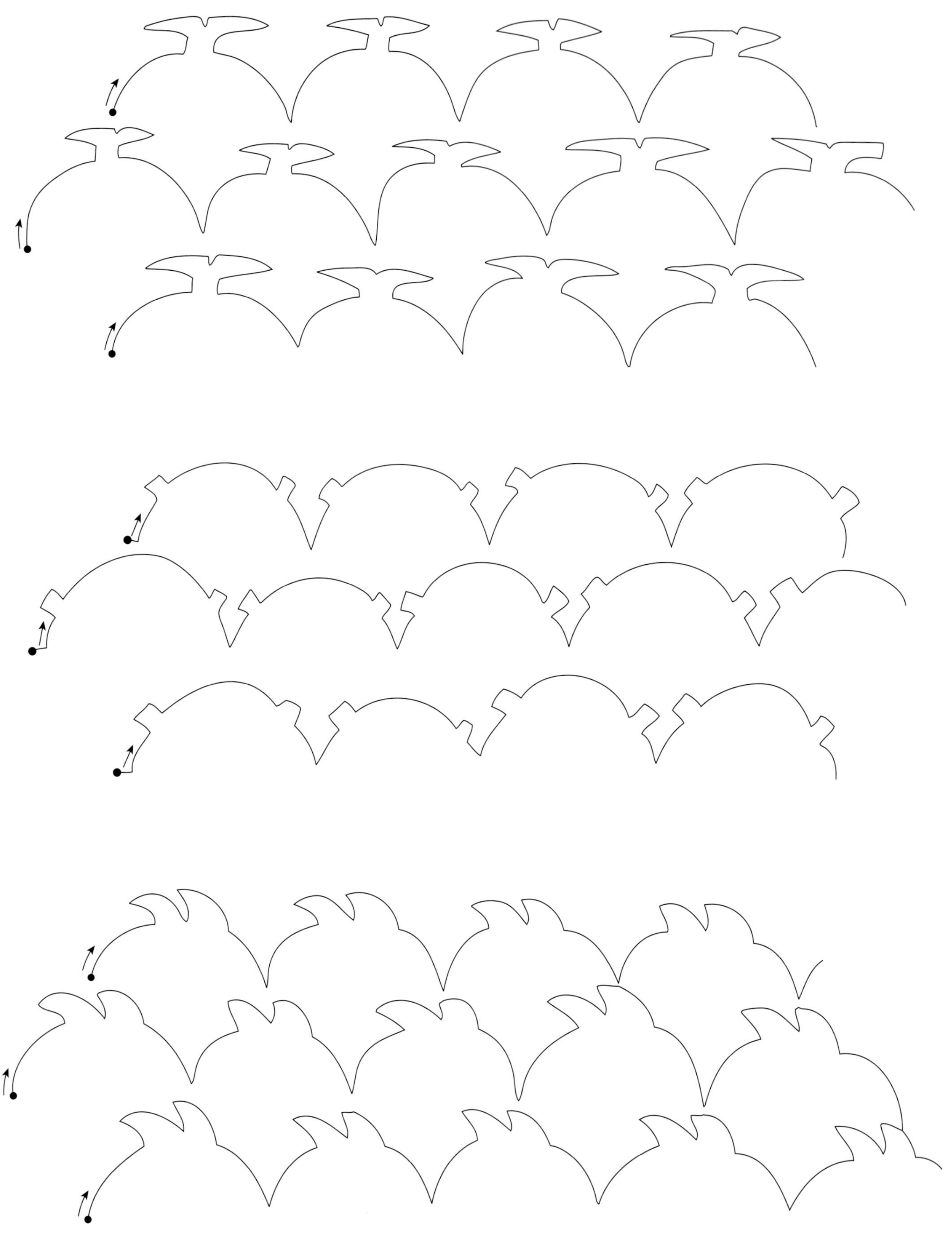

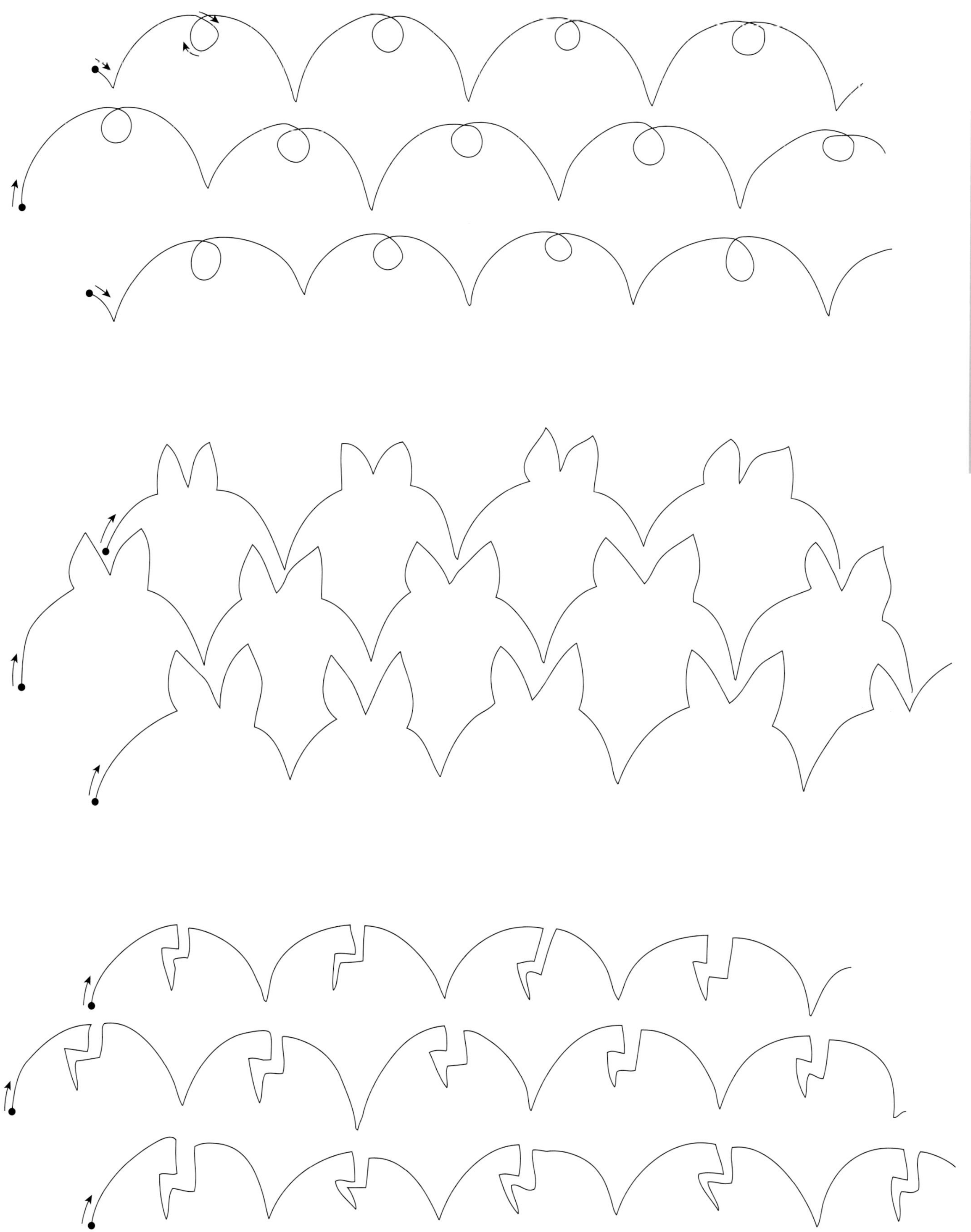

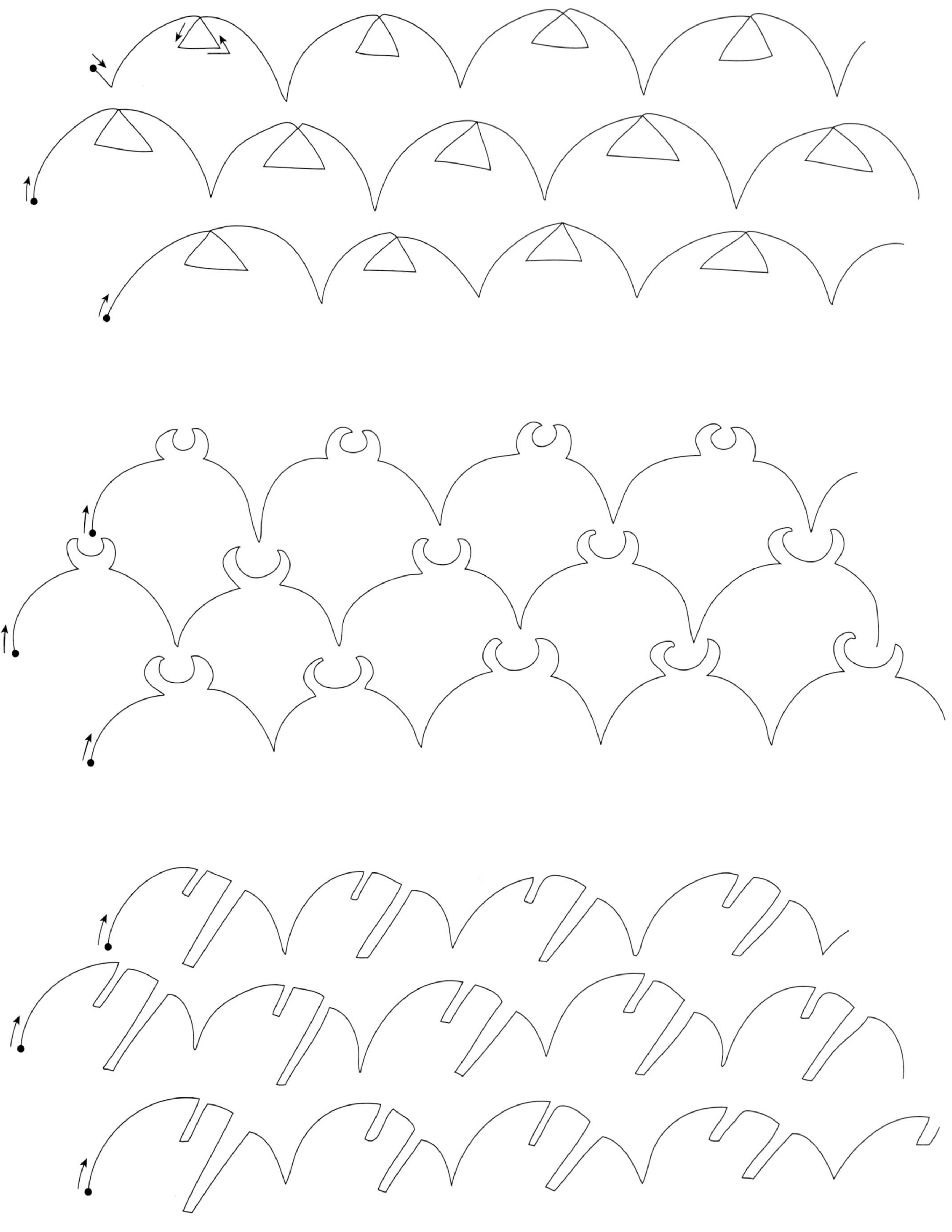

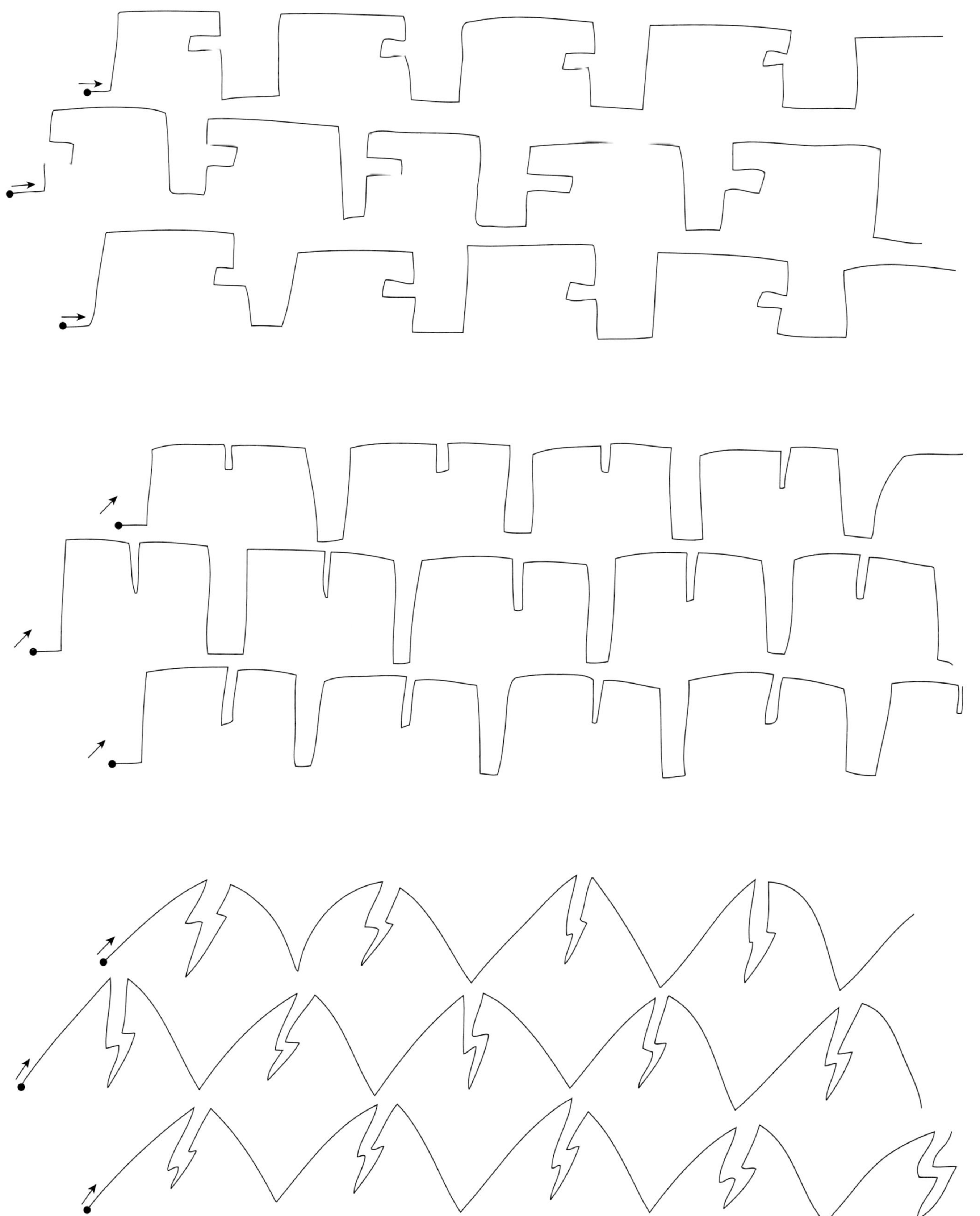

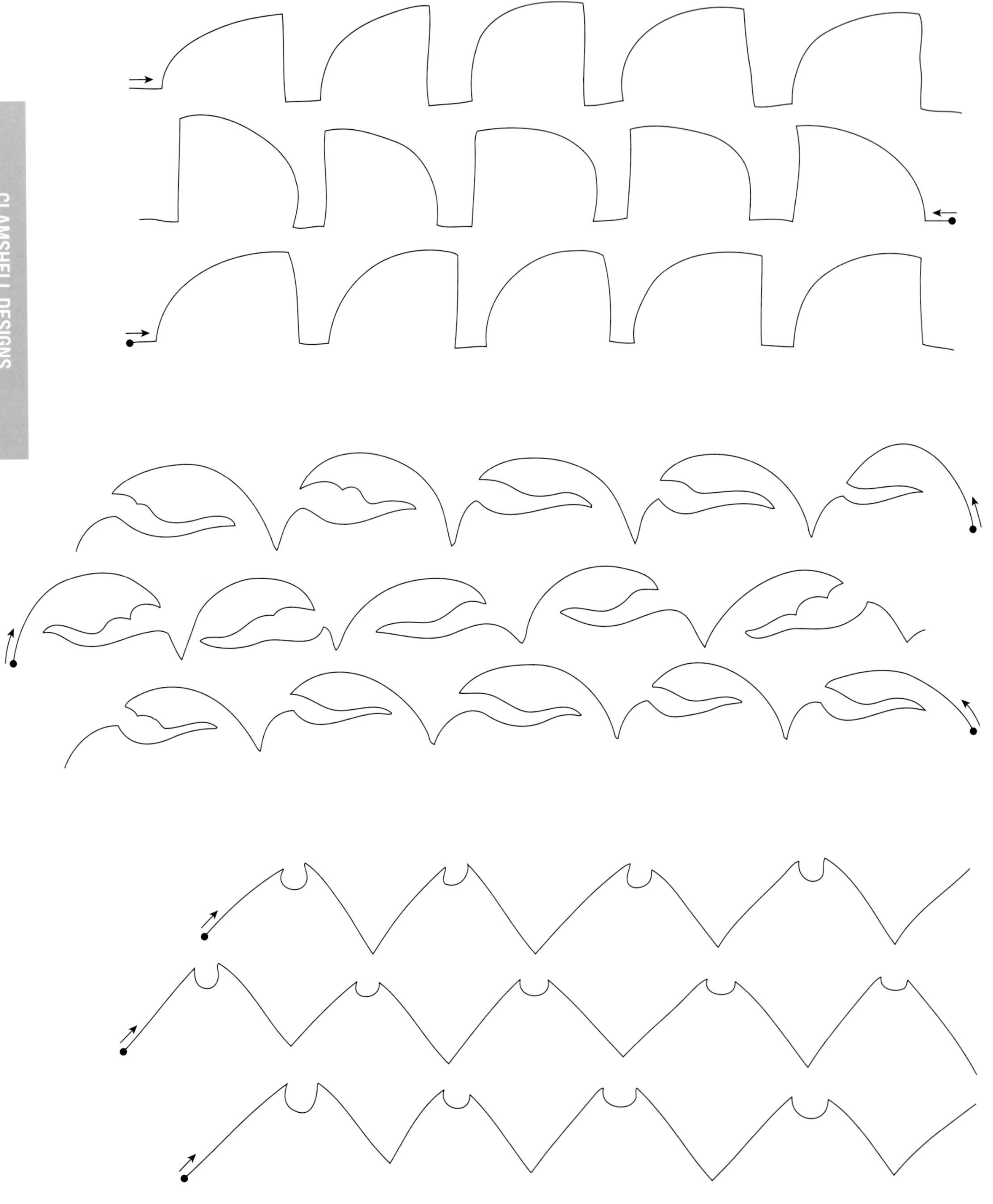

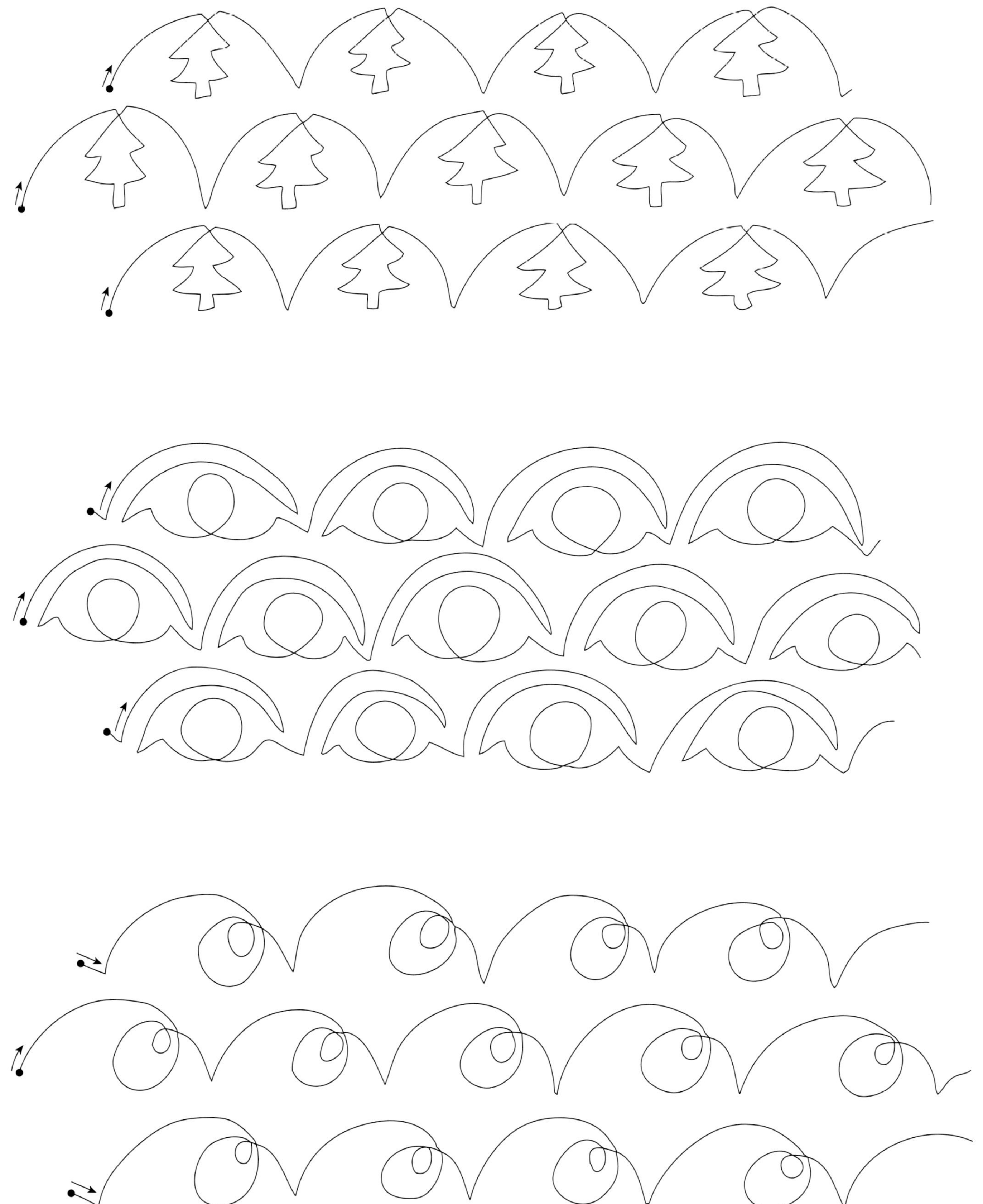

CLAMSHELL DESIGNS

CLAMSHELL DESIGNS

CLAMSHELL DESIGNS

Wave Designs

AN INTRODUCTION TO WAVES

Look at the wave as a format for drawing new designs. Waves have the same negative space on both sides. Wave designs are often used to fill borders. Wave designs can be identical repeating rows, or offset in alternating rows.

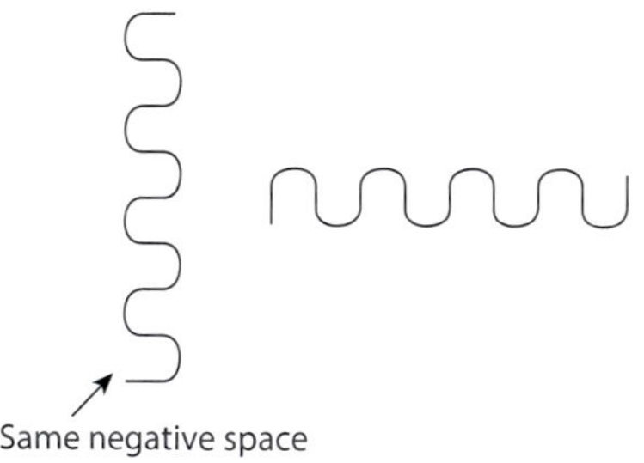

The offset row

Single wave for a narrow border, or two offset rows for a wider space

Start with a classic row of waves, and add a small or elaborate variation.

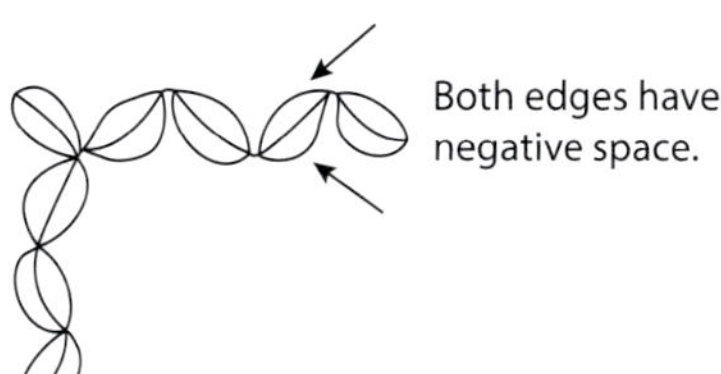

A bit of exaggeration will turn a classic wave into a rope design.

WAVE DESIGNS

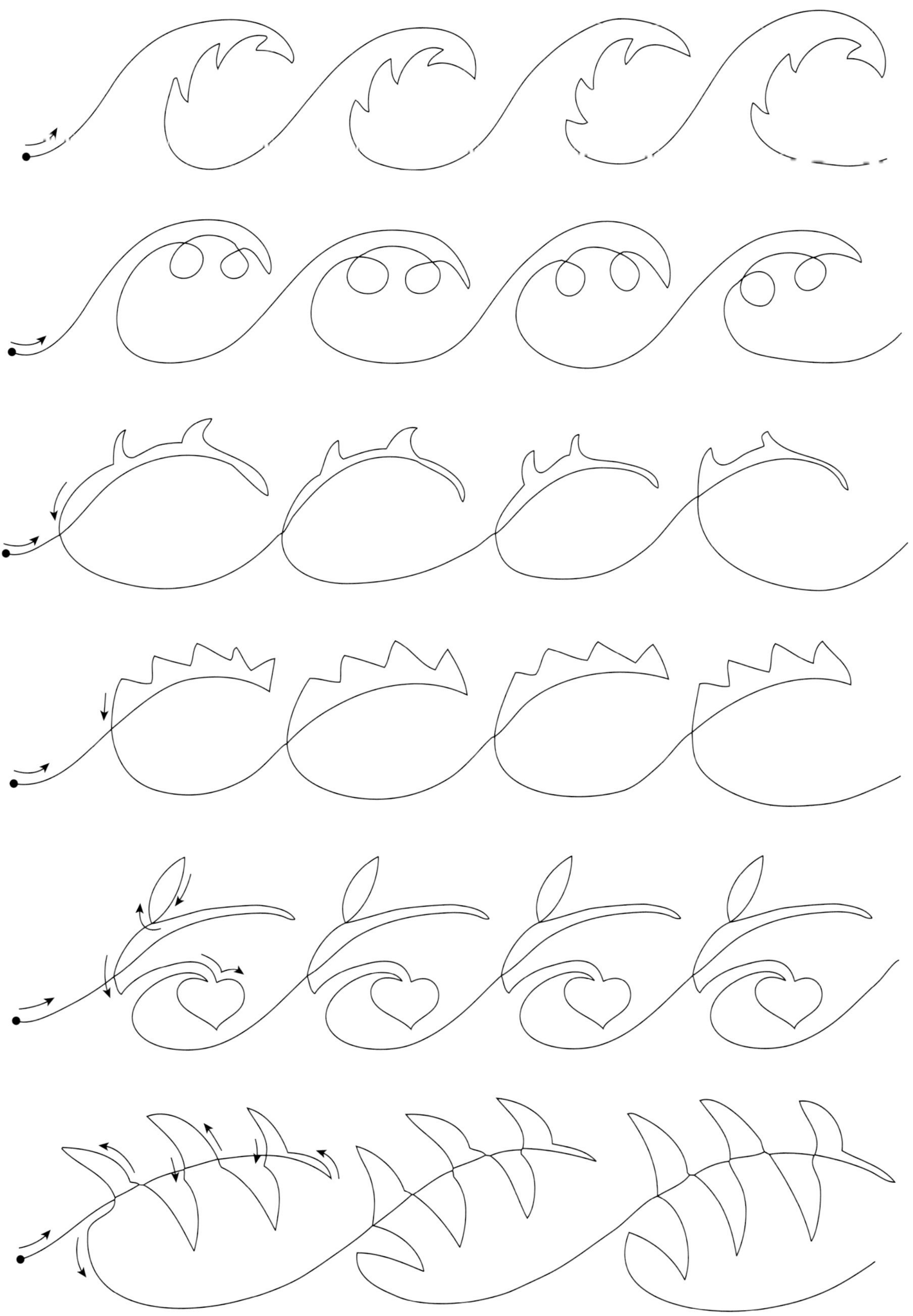

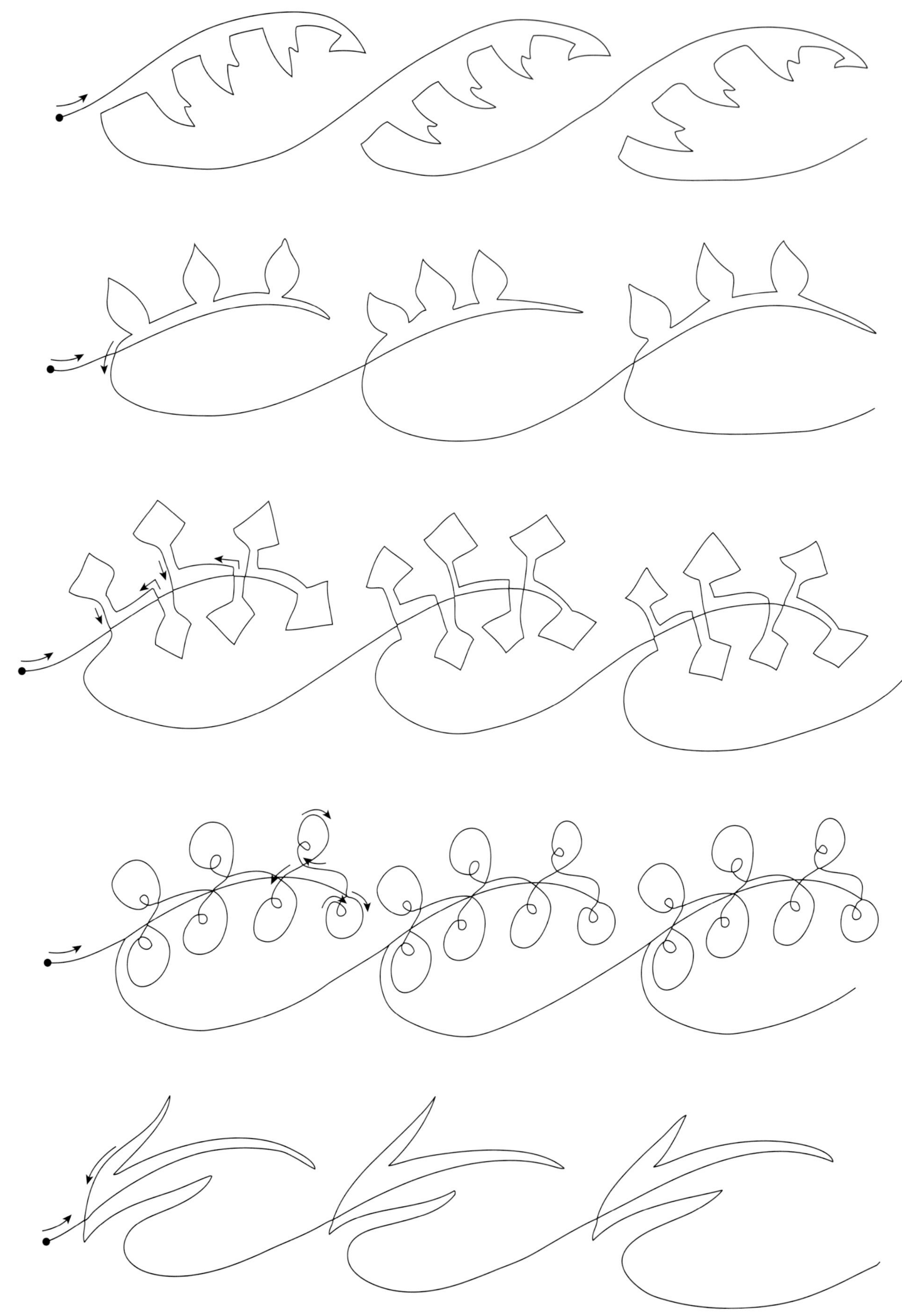

WAVE DESIGNS

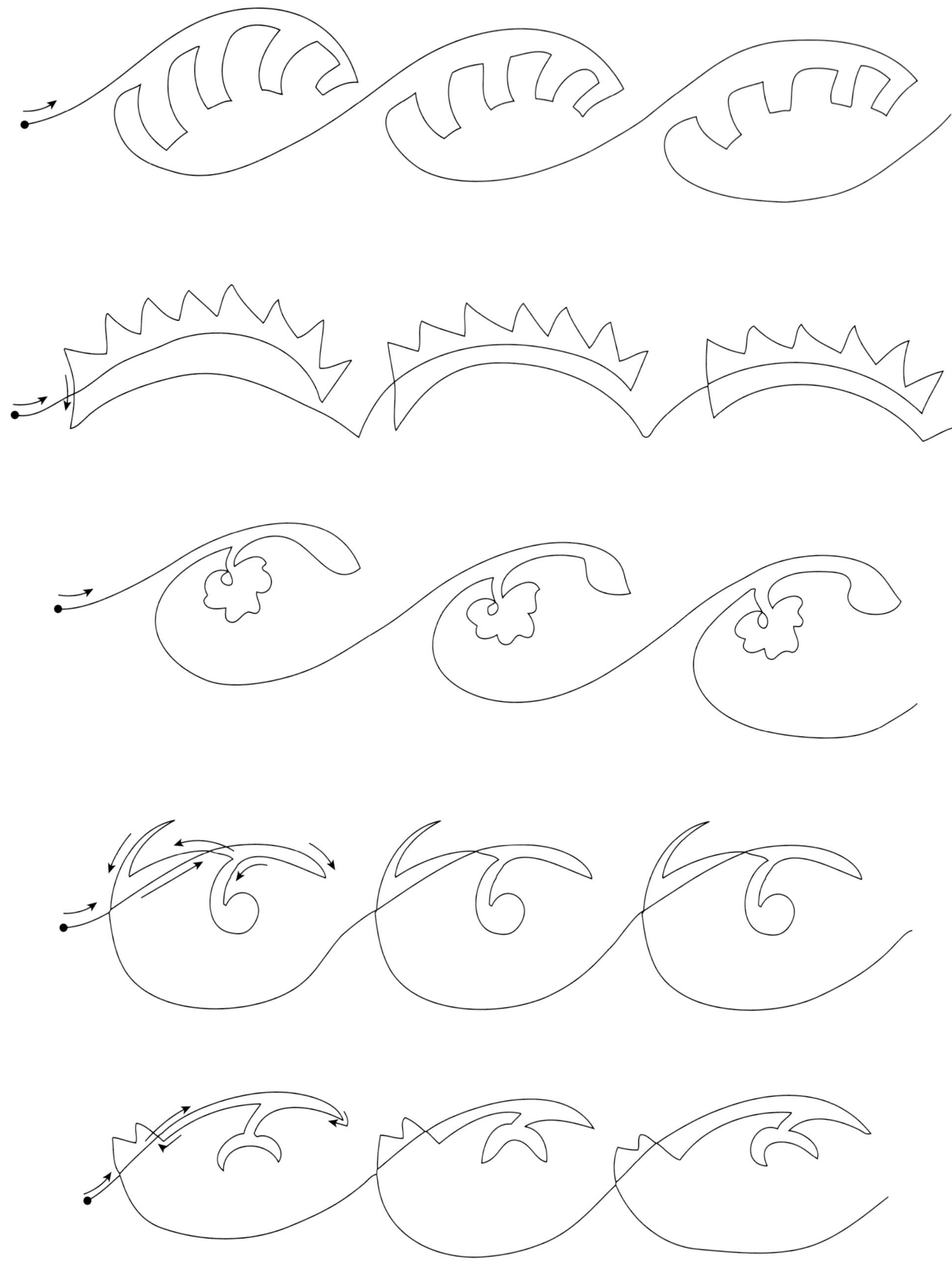

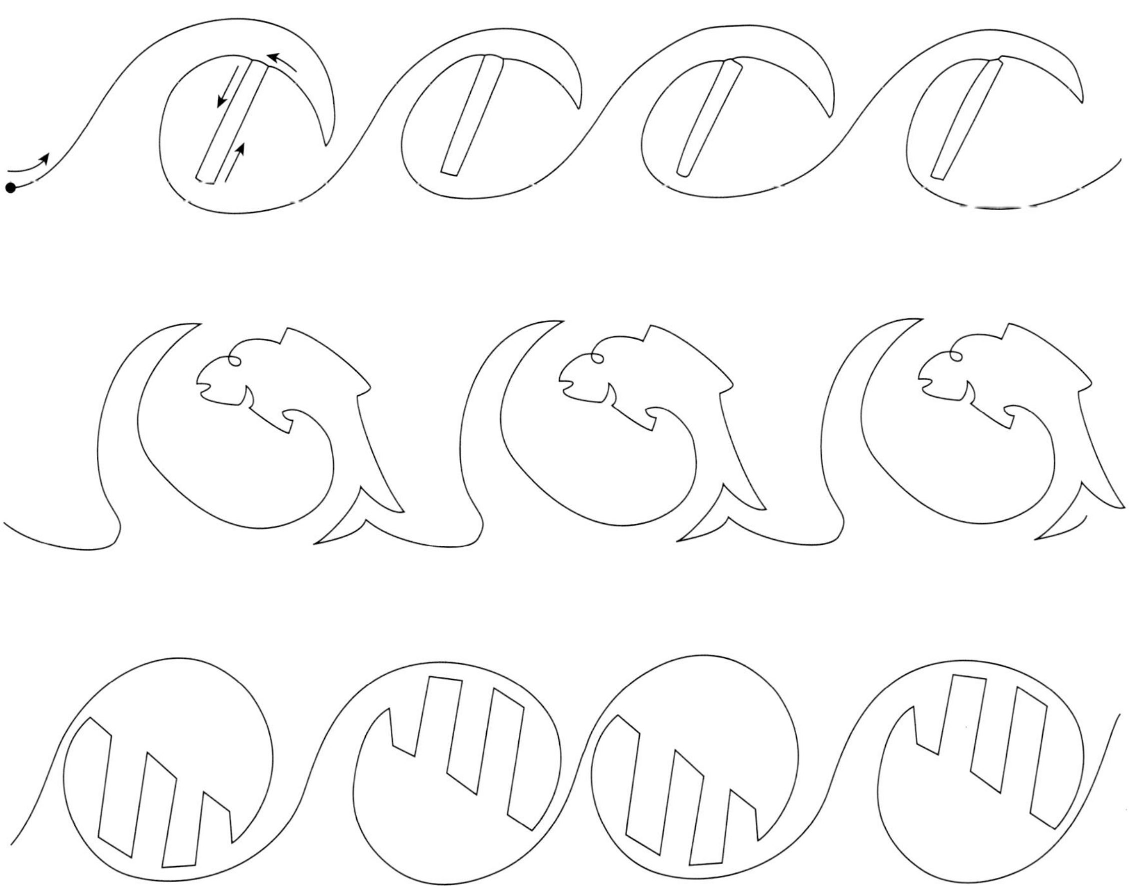

Serpentine Designs

AN INTRODUCTION TO SERPENTINES

Serpentine lines are often used as a spine for creating feather designs, but there are some excellent examples of other ways to make use of such a simple format.

For example, this shallow-humped serpentine has an "accidental" leaf detail that's perfect for a ¾″–1″ border.

The leaf detail does more than decorate the line. It also distracts you from noticing whether or not the curves are precisely measured and matched. As a fan of the human touch, I tend to make a distinction between the concept of perfection and precision.

SERPENTINE DESIGNS

Fan Designs

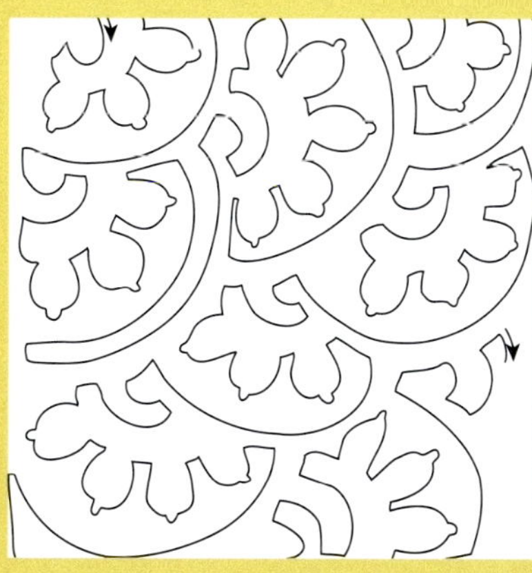

AN INTRODUCTION TO FANS

I particularly like designing with the Baptist Fan as a basis. It is one of the most-recognized classic patterns, usually traveling at random across a quilt. To draw it, trace against the edge of a plate to get an arc, move the plate down, and draw against it again just inside that arc. To make it travel fluidly in machine quilting, begin at the center of the nesting arcs, with the smallest arc. Continue an arc until it "hits" another line or an edge of the quilt, echo that line or edge for a short distance—½″ maybe—and begin the next arc.

Always keep going until you bump against that next field. Just shy of the collision I stop, at a distance equal to the space between arcs. When complete, this creates the illusion of another arc. When you choose, otherwise, to go completely to the next line, the sewn result is a consistent yet intermittent double-line quilting area. Neither is right or wrong, but make it a choice, not an accident.

Here is a visual comparison:

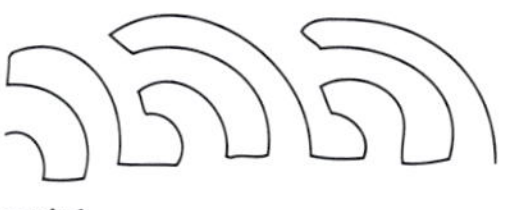

With space

Double line areas

To make the Baptist Fan travel across a quilt as a random overall pattern, start from the smallest arc and make the concentric arcs until they are no longer smooth to sew. When you reach a size that wobbles instead of arcs, start a new small center arc. By the second or third time you start a new "rainbow" you will start to see "valleys" to use for your starting places. Do not make a loop or a hook unless it is part of an intended variation. Just make a smaller version of the same shape. Any extra turns of the line will look out of place—though, of course, with beauty and repetition that will become its own pattern.

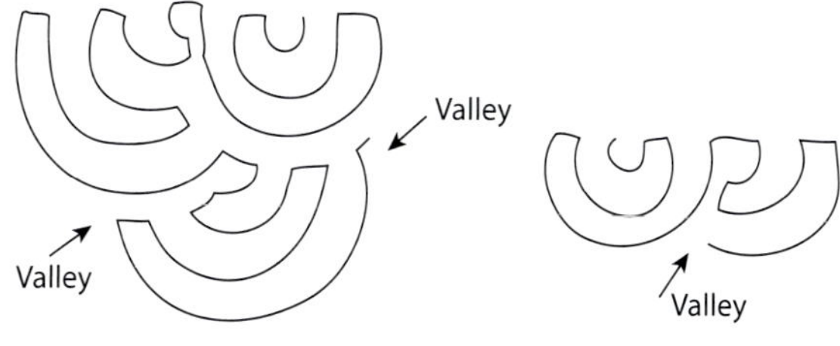

The design to the right illustrates some difficulties for a flowing overall pattern; the long petal fills space so quickly there's no room to wiggle over to another area in pattern. Either a doubled center arc, or an extra-long reach or a hooked echo will get you out of a tight spot.

FAN DESIGNS

Feather Designs

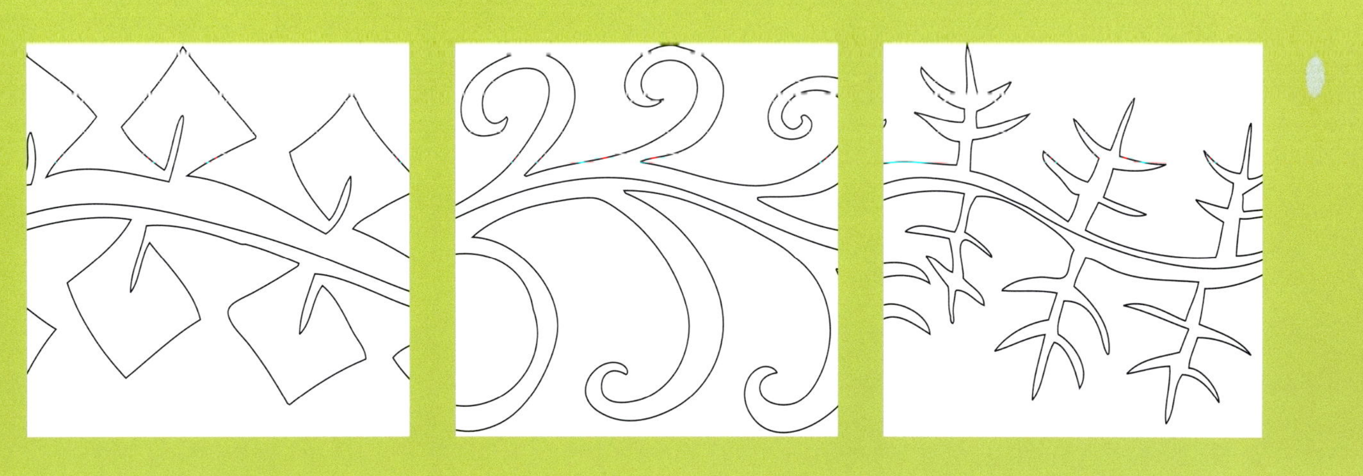

AN INTRODUCTION TO FEATHERS

The classic feather quilting design is much loved by those who feel precision is equal to perfection. I lean more toward finding perfection in the unique and askew production of the unsteady, but searching, hand. So, let that thought launch this study of the feather as a format—not a pattern. Feather designs have a curvy spine with plumes on both sides of the spine. Much has been written about making those plumes in the most aesthetic shape but I'll show you ideas that will launch you into finding yet more variations for those plumes than I can put to paper here.

A shallow curve works no matter the space of the spine. The plumes will reach to the right edges of the border, no matter how shallow or deep the curve. In a wide border, a deep spine will work too. Spines can also flow and curve to fit a block, and then the plumes can fill the space.

Shallow spine

Deep spine

Feather block designs

FEATHER DESIGNS

A precise plume will nest into the next, and will have a voluptuous tip and a long trailing tail virtually echoing the spine.

It can be a mental juggle to make one side of plumes left to right and the other side right to left. If any of the following designs are difficult to stitch with one spine, just double it.

FEATHER DESIGNS

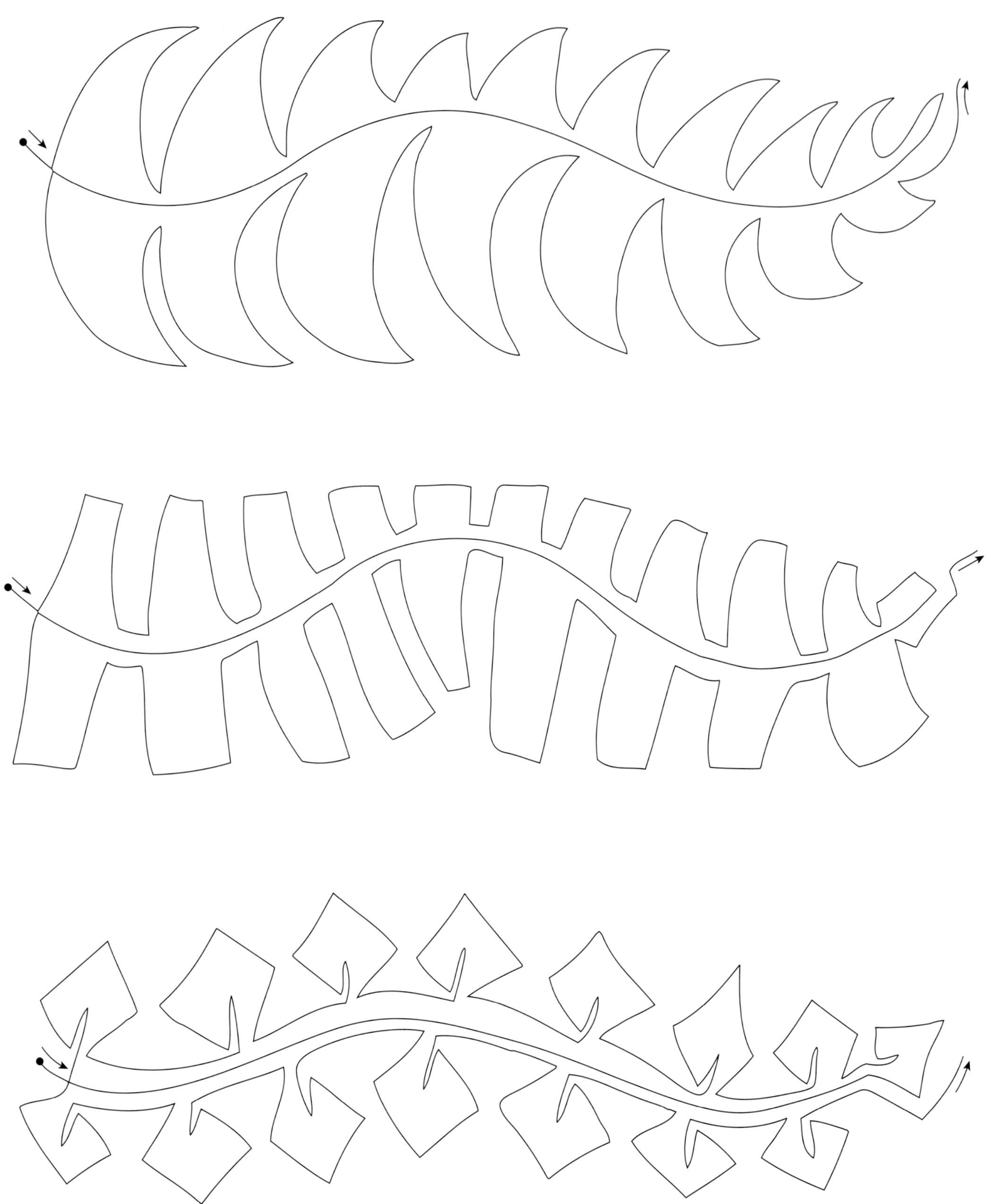

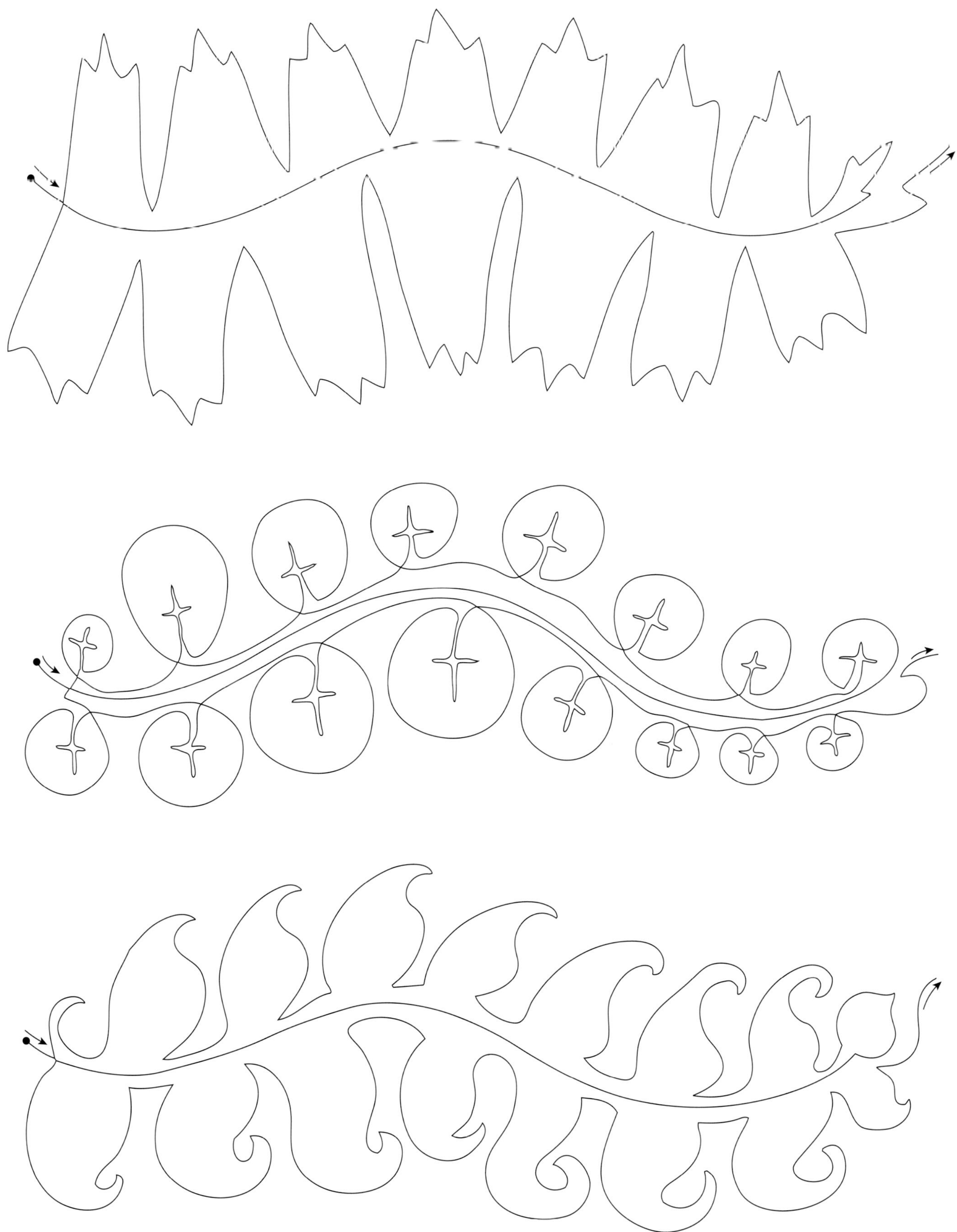

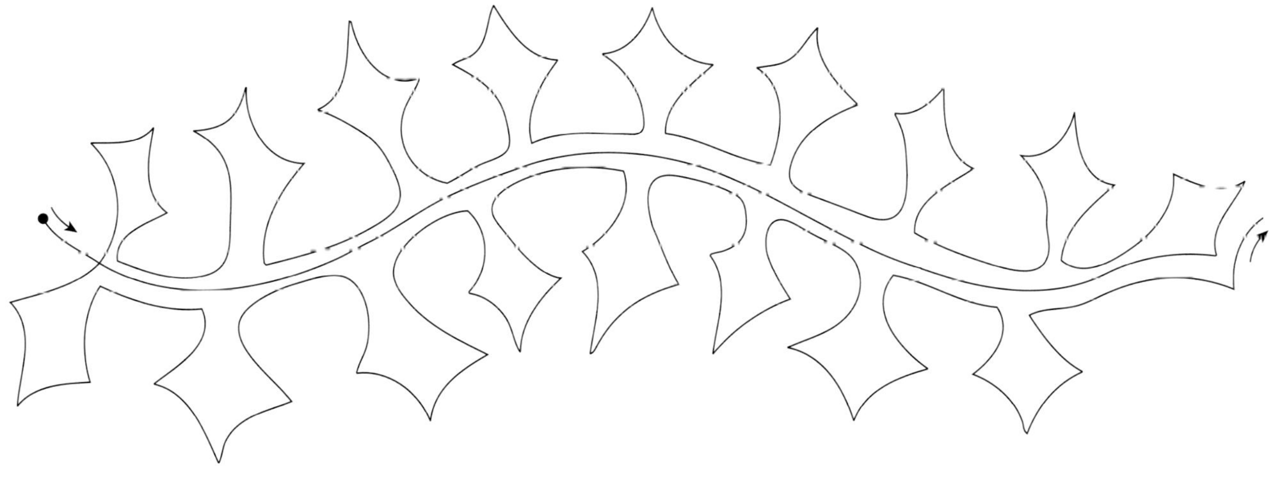

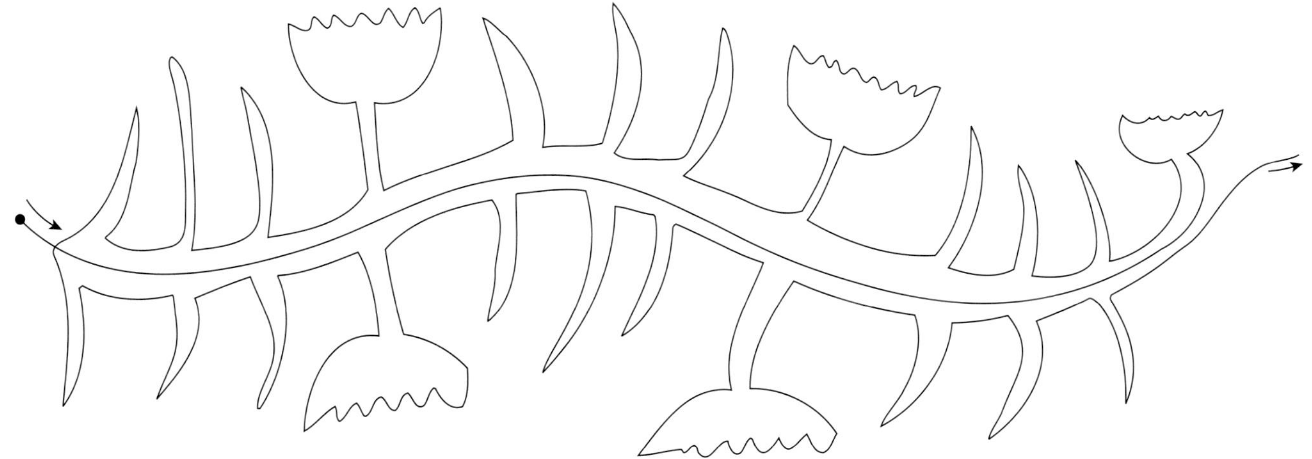

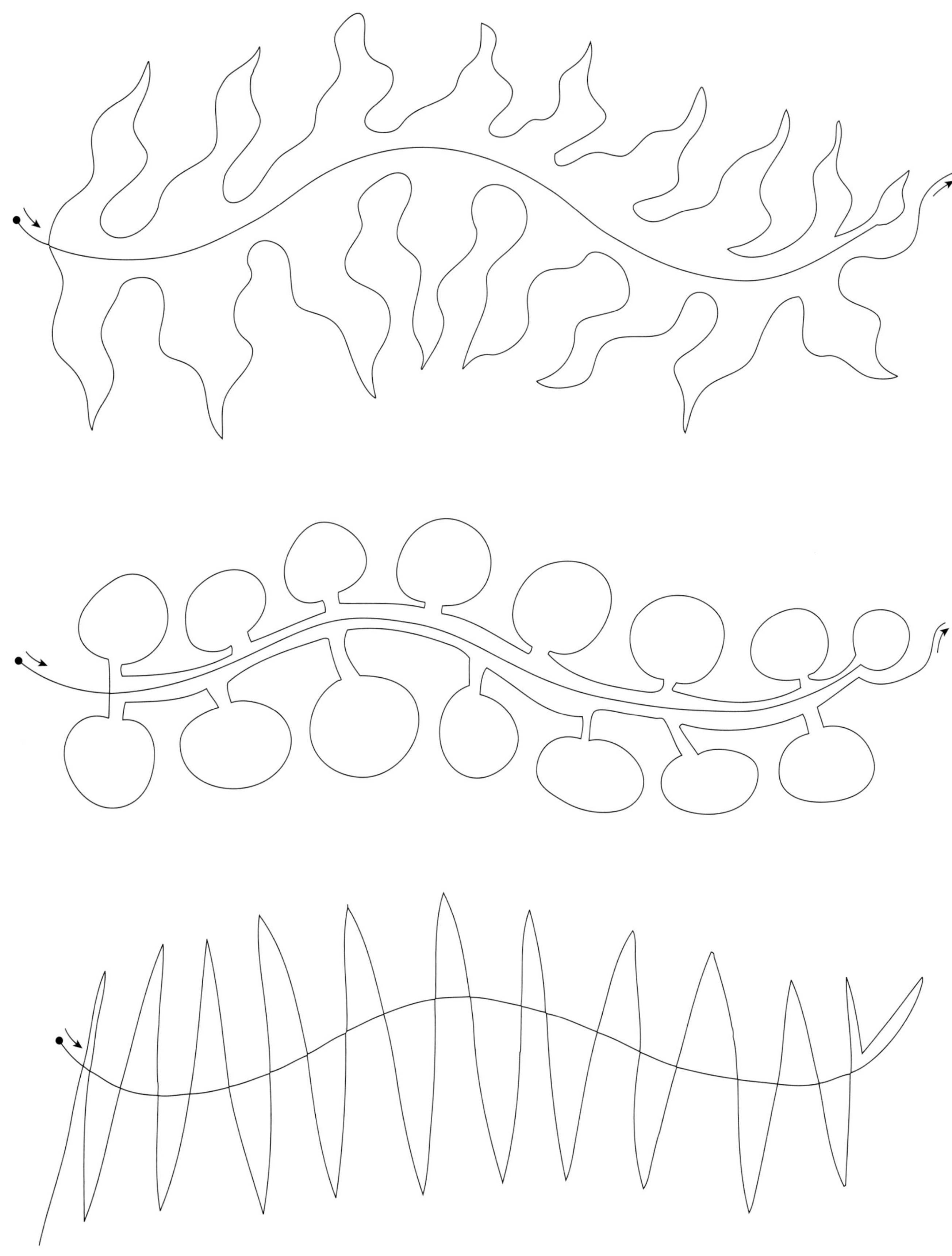

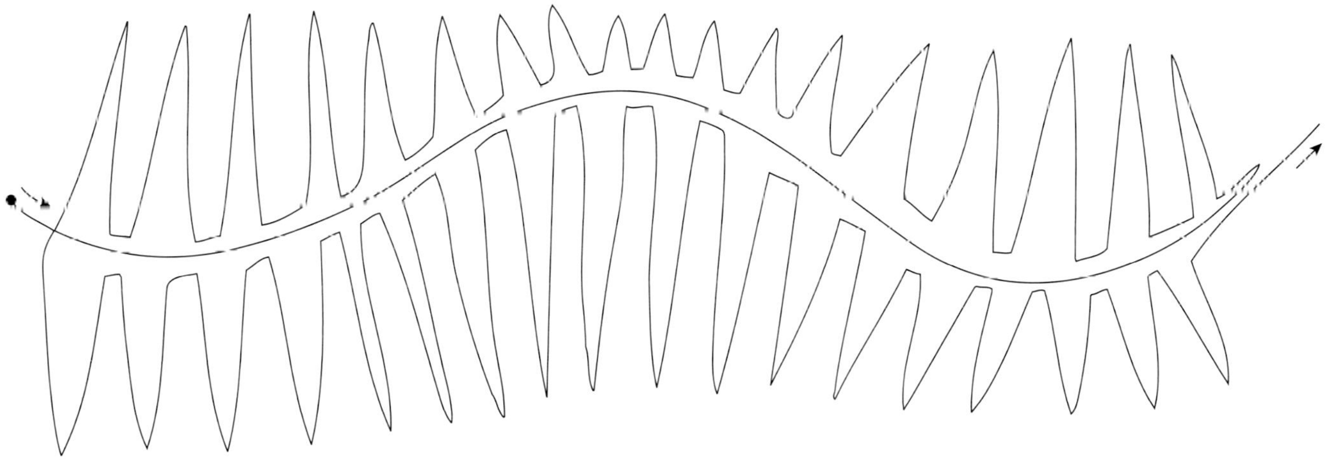

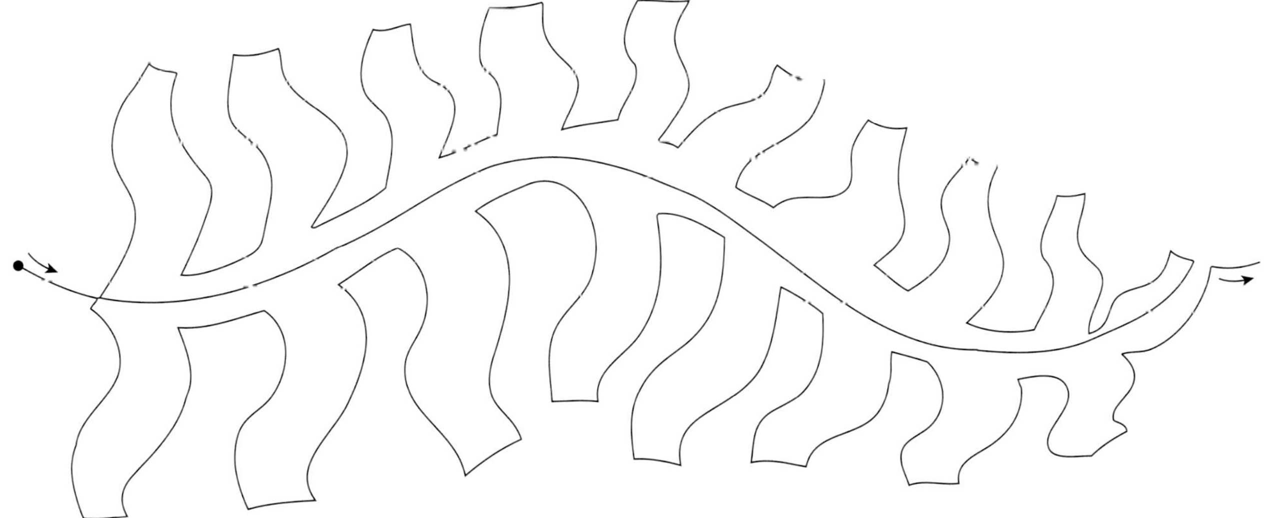

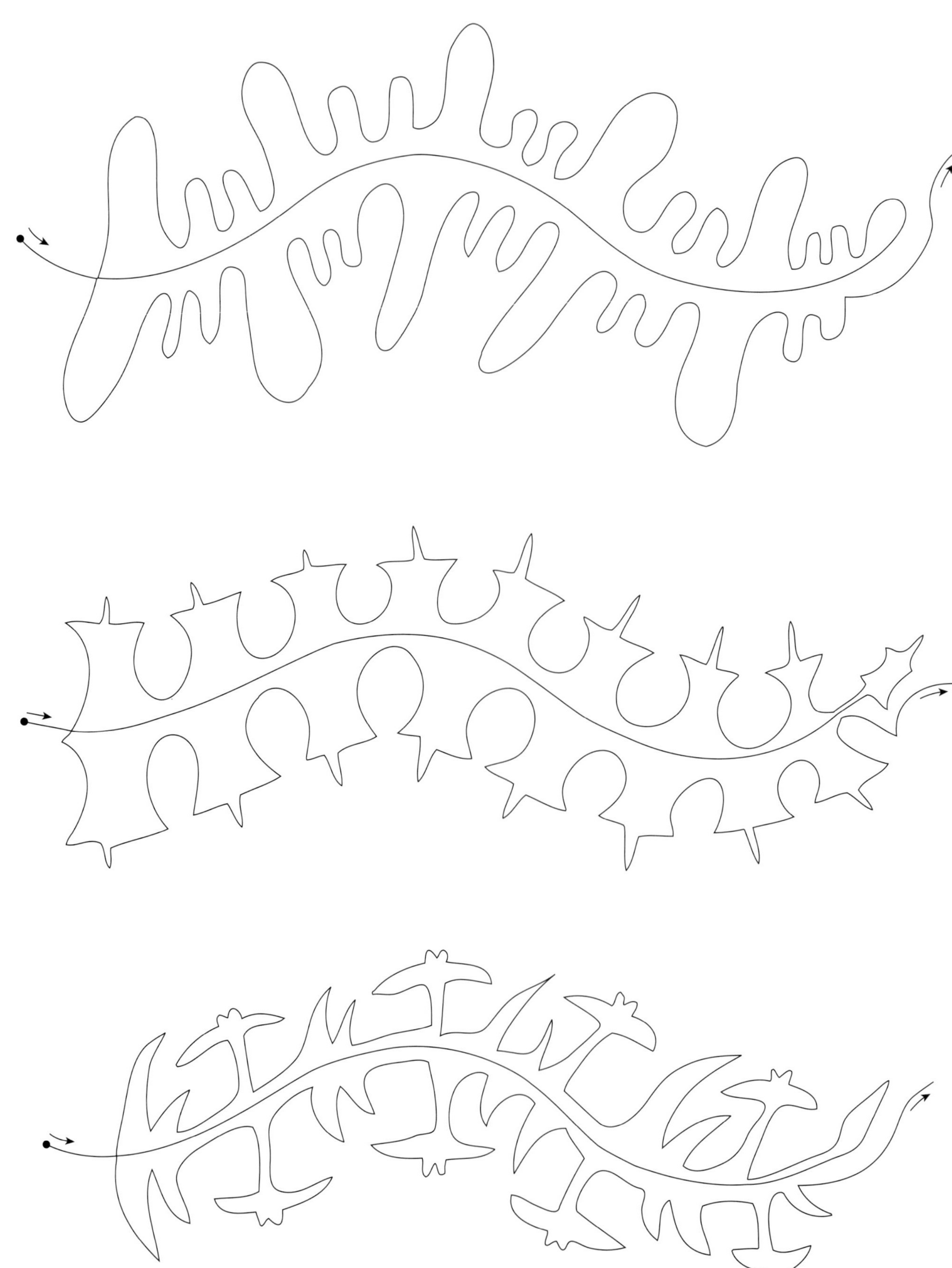

500 PICTORIAL DESIGNS

Birds

BIRDS

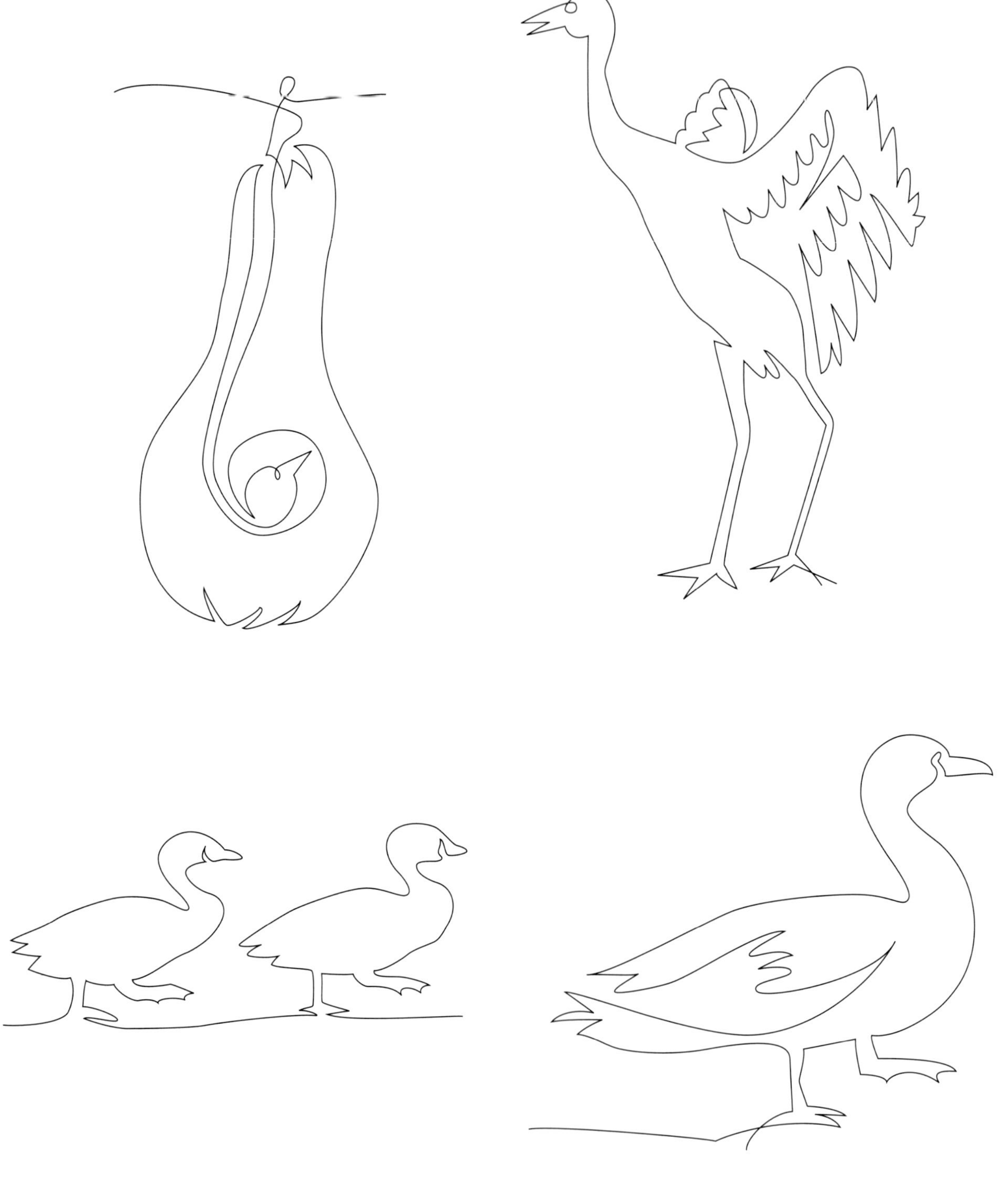

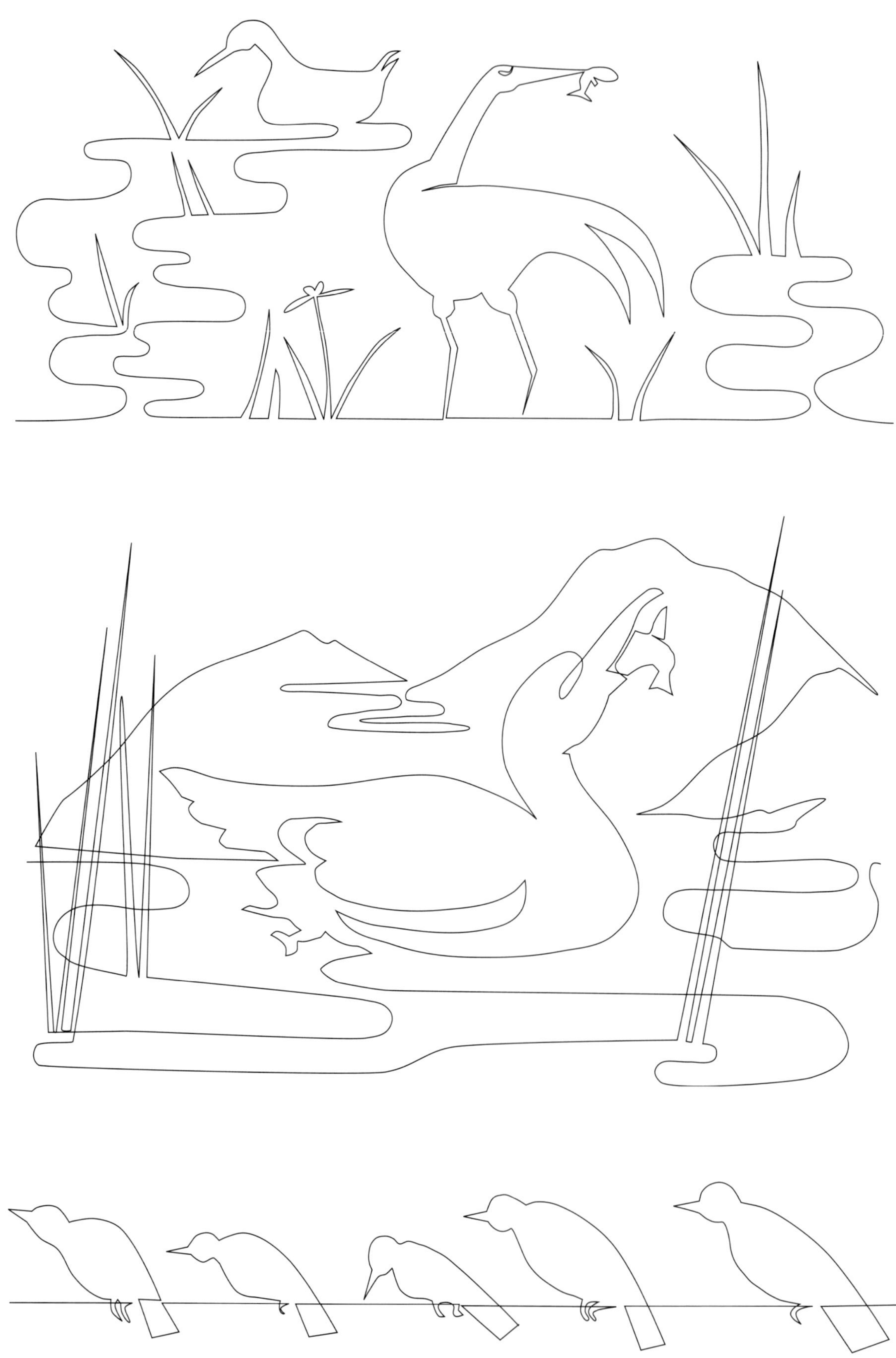

Fungi and Insects

In the Garden

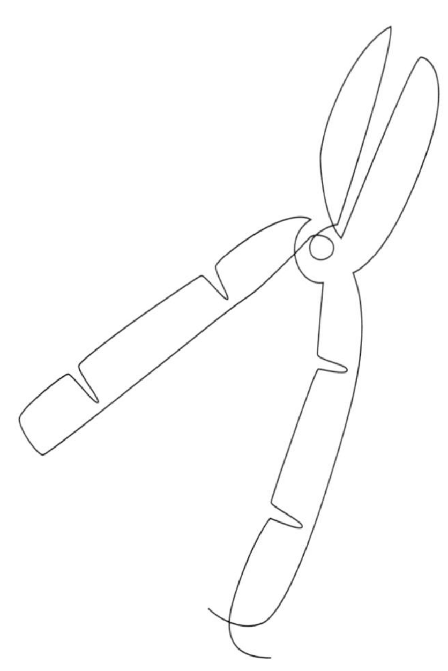

On the Farm

The Wilderness File

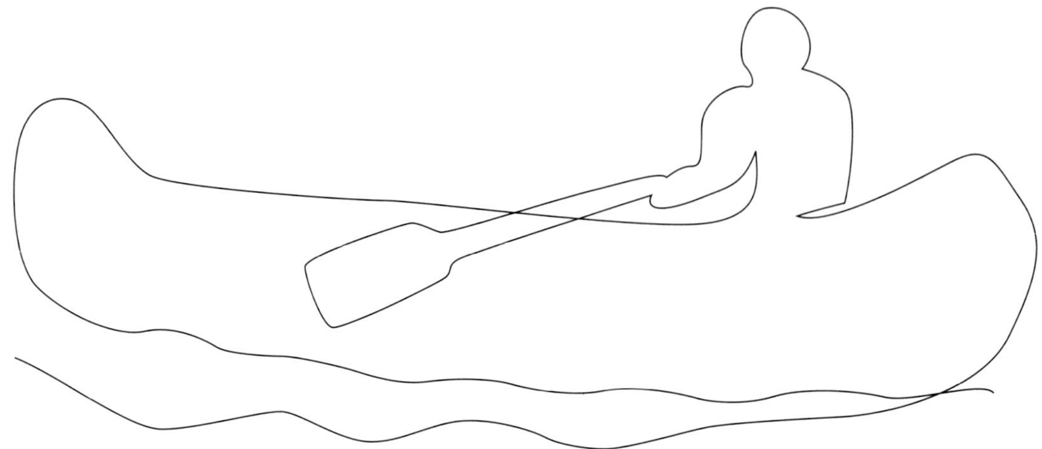

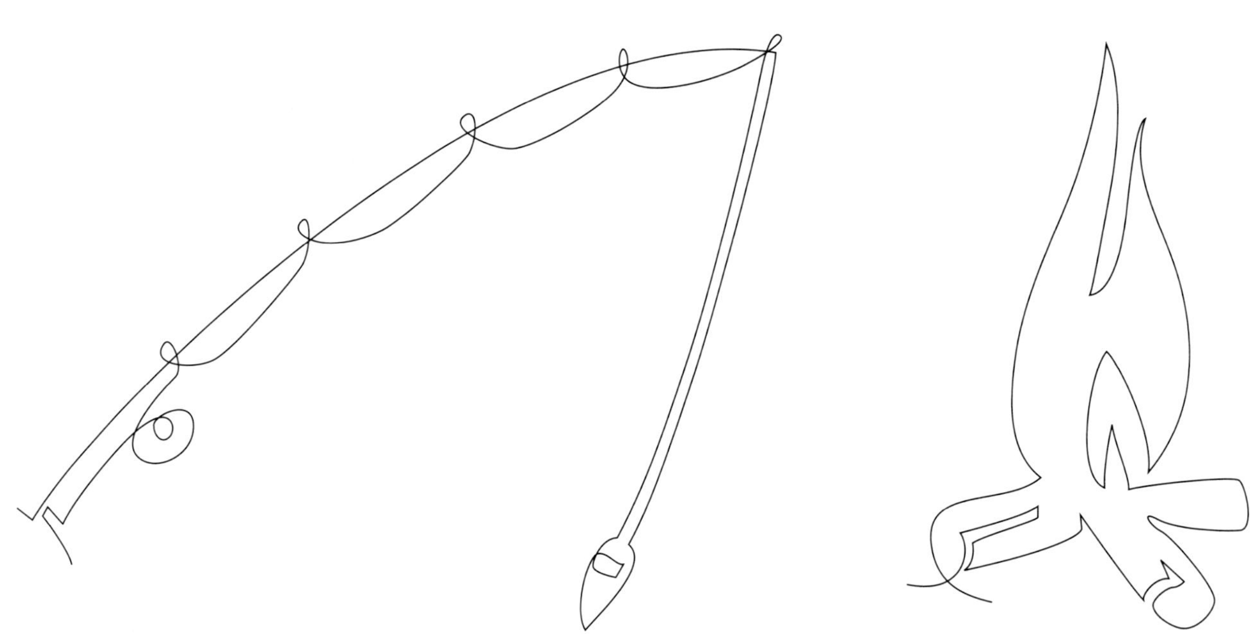

Staying at Home

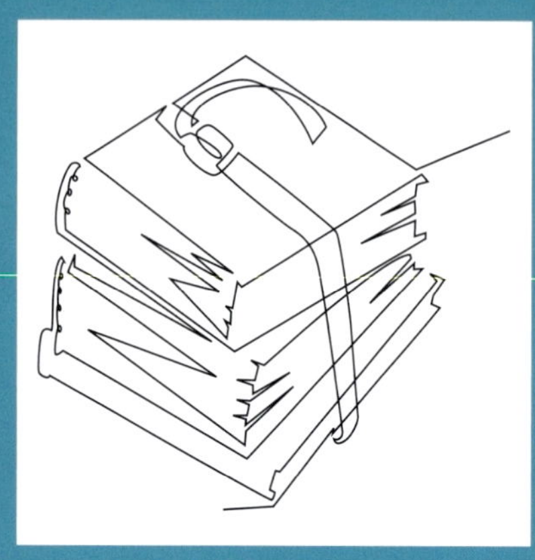

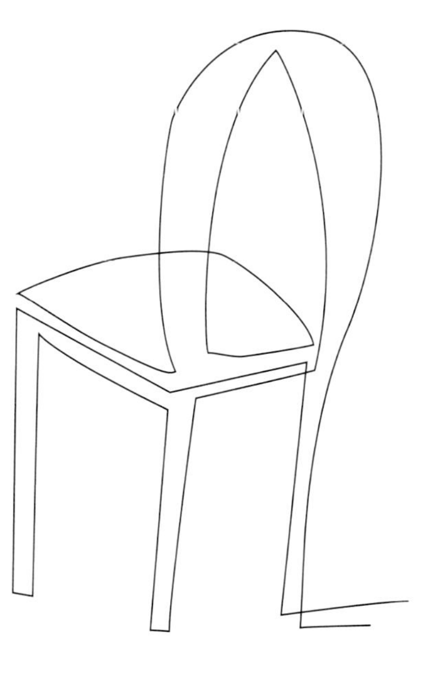

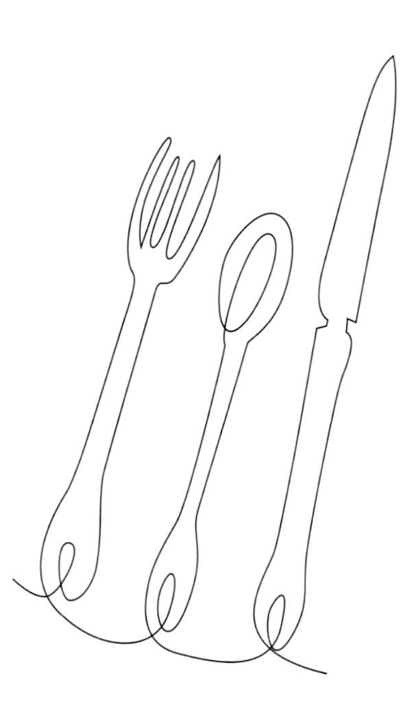

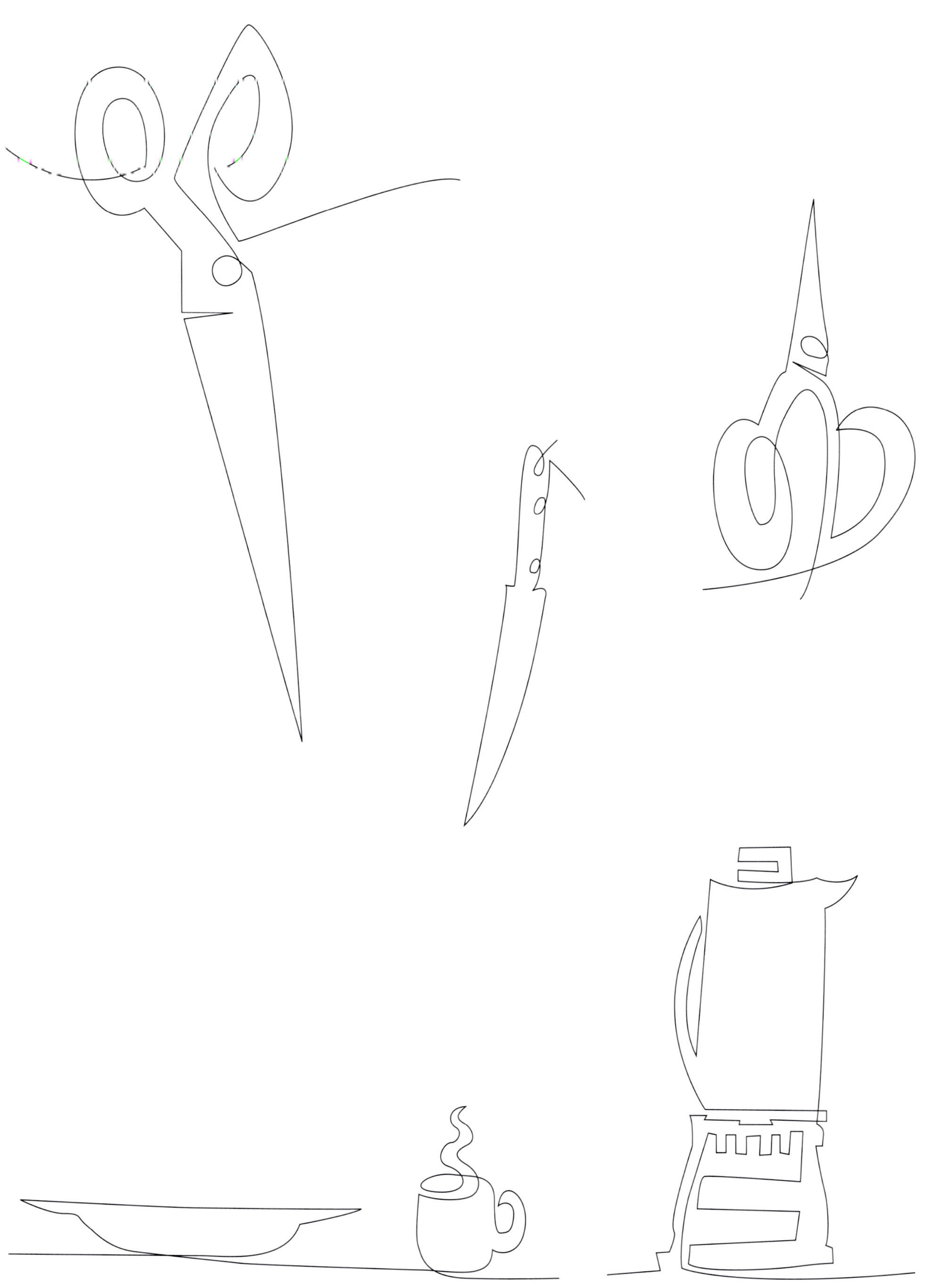

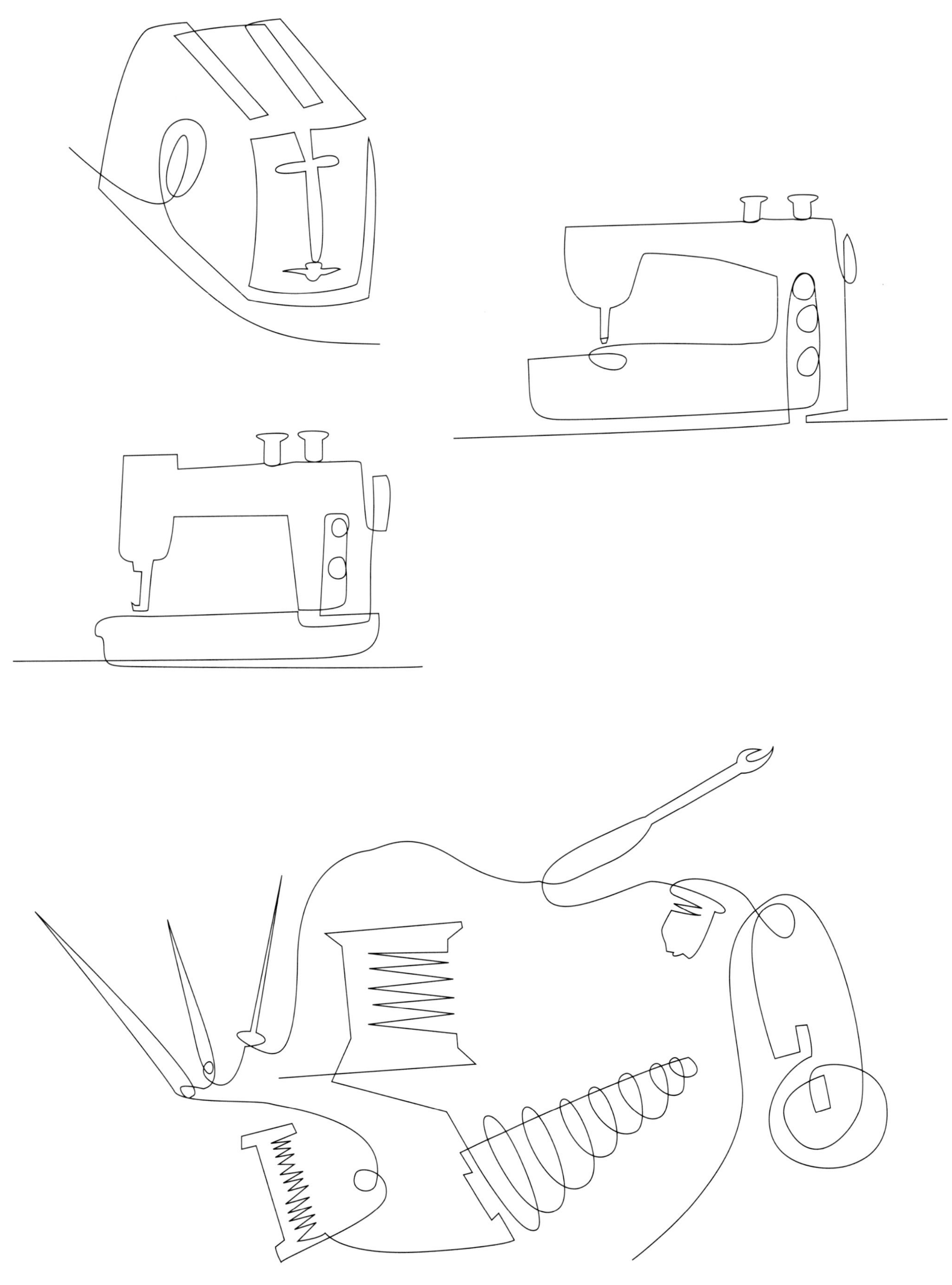

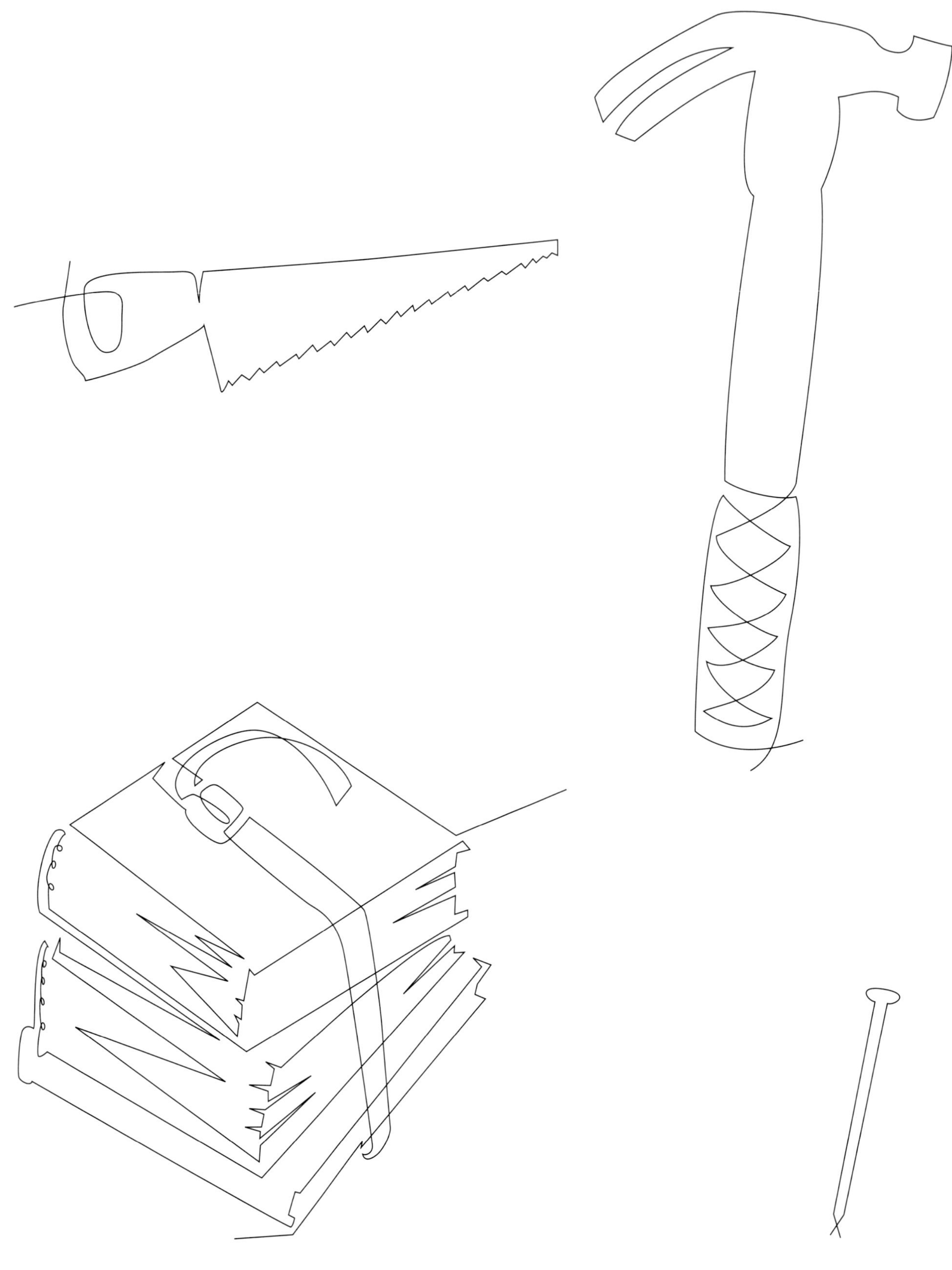

STAYING AT HOME

Out At Sea

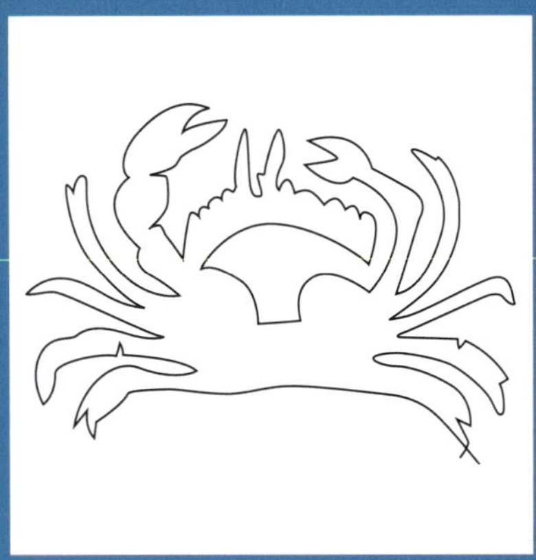

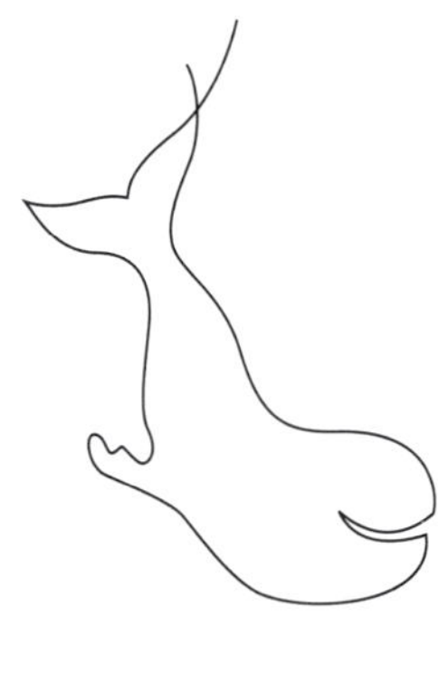

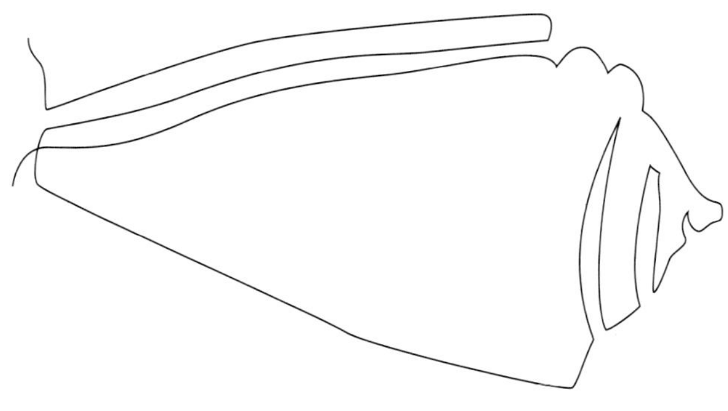

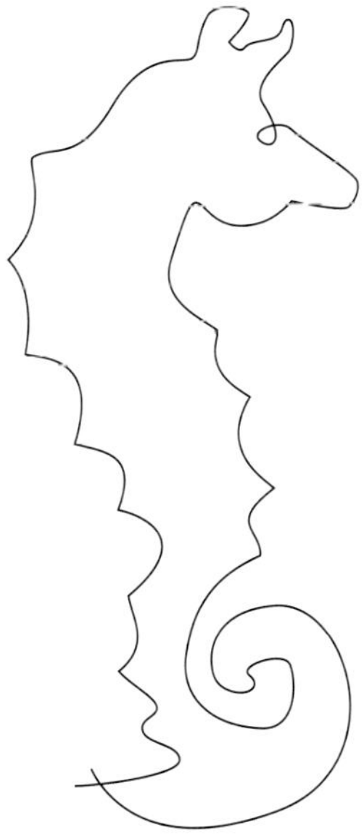

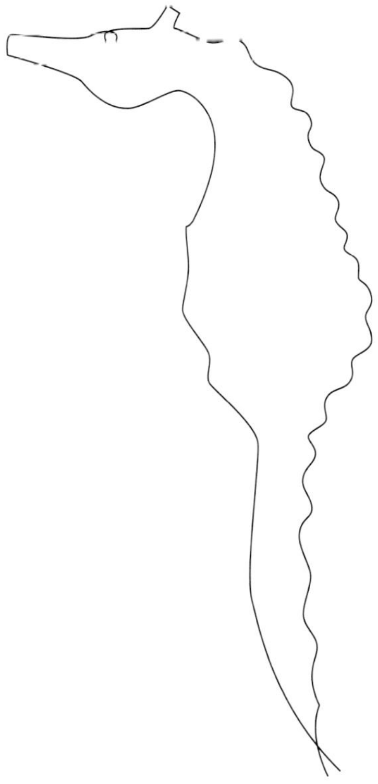

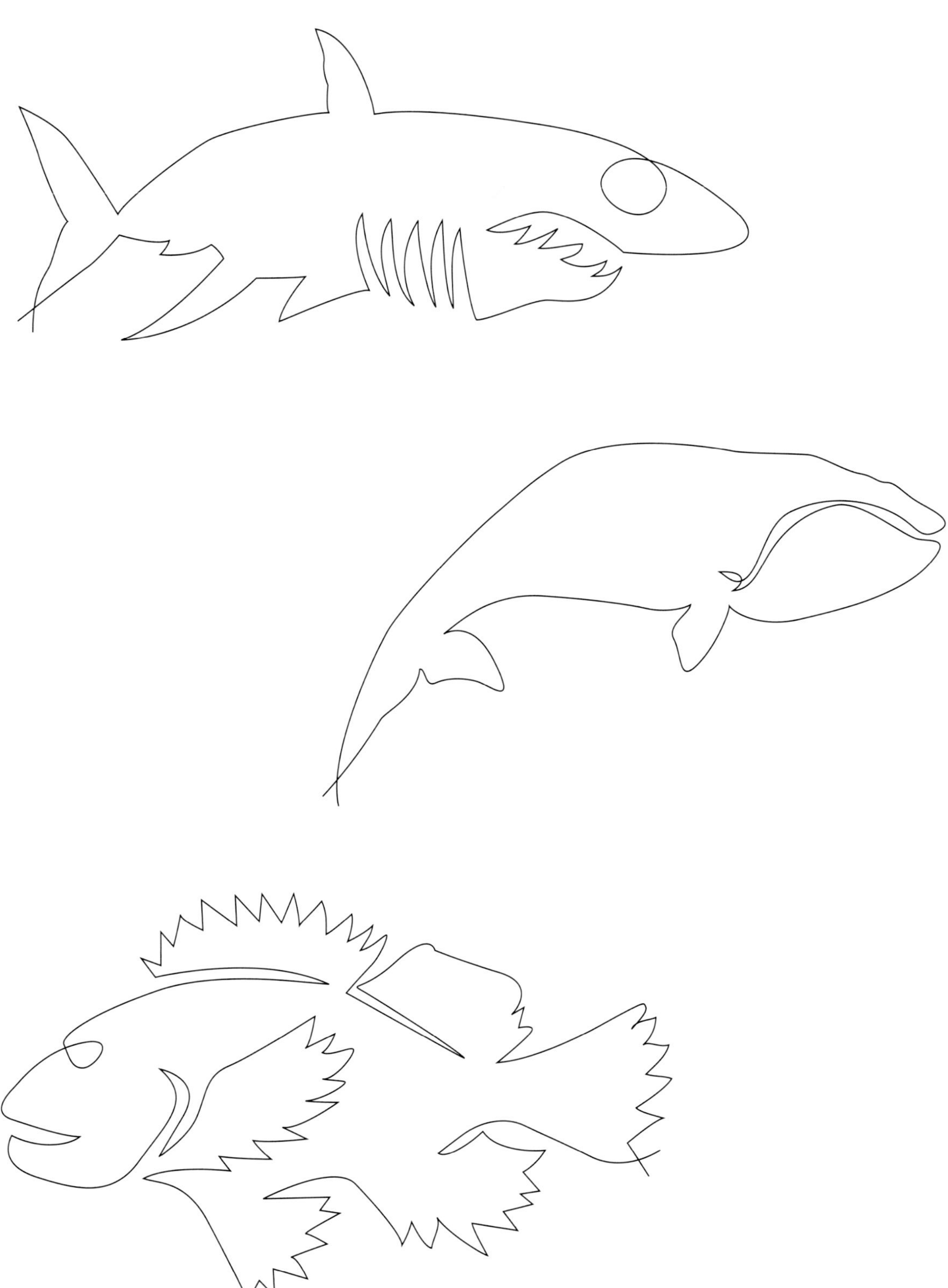

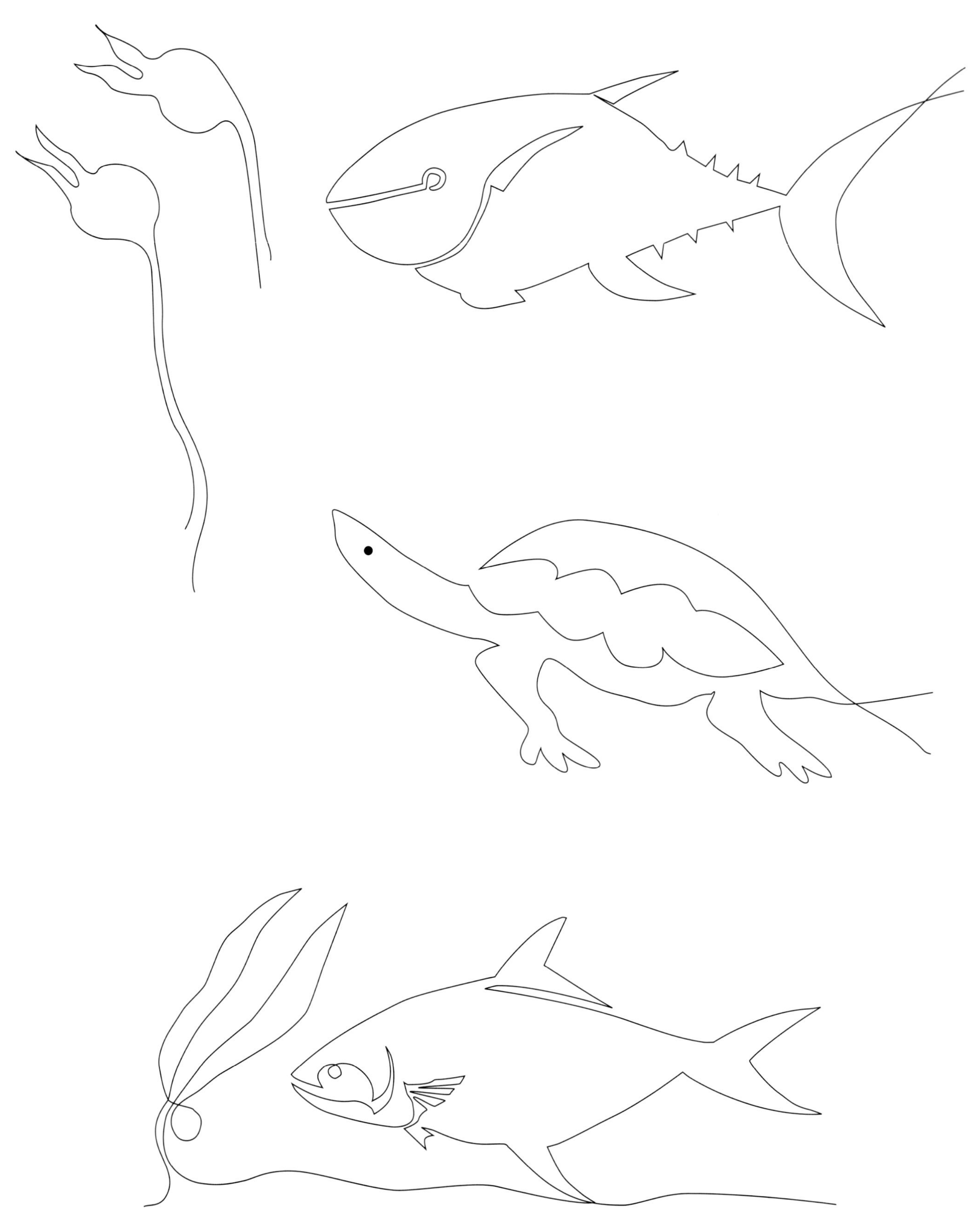

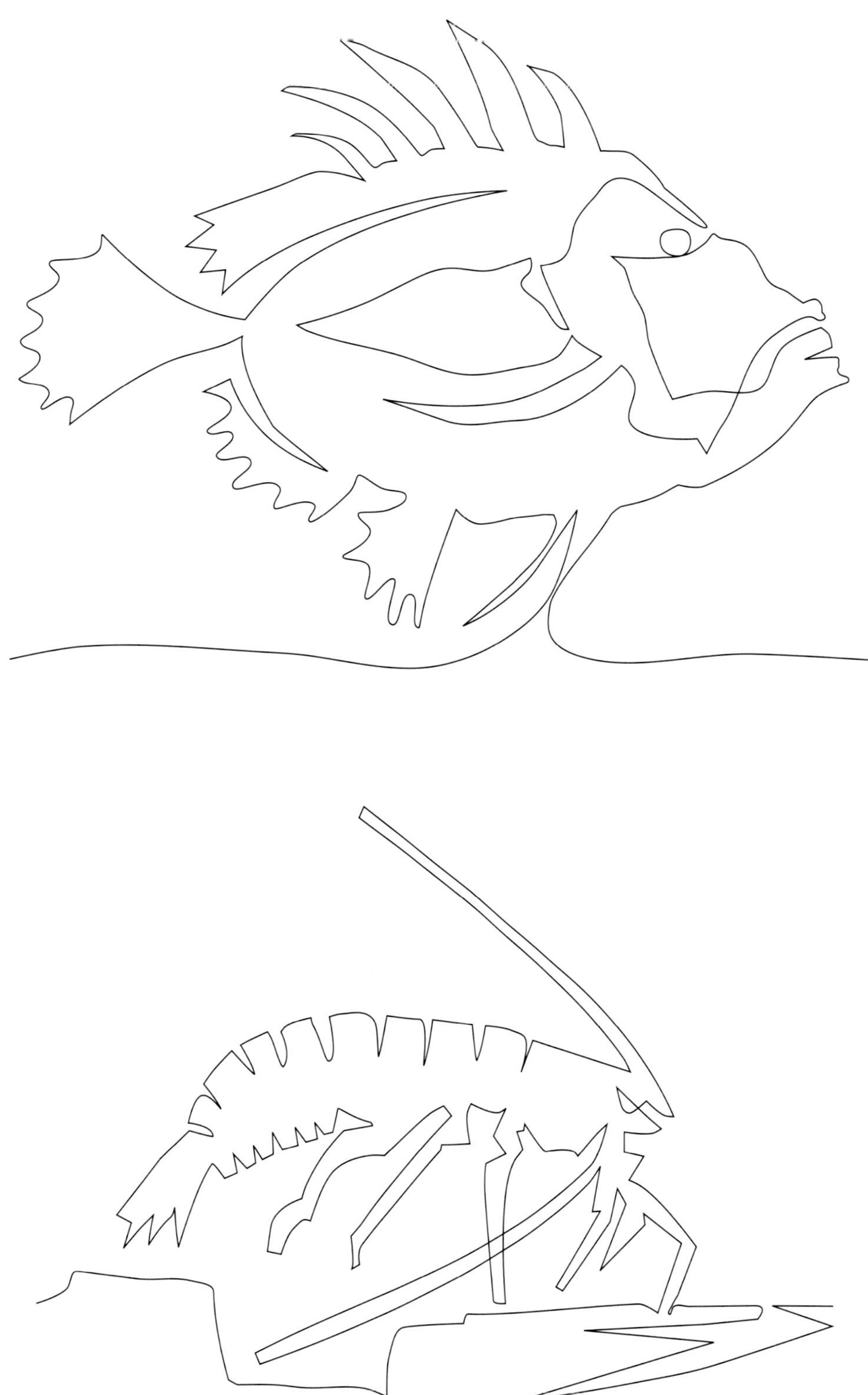

Through the Seasons

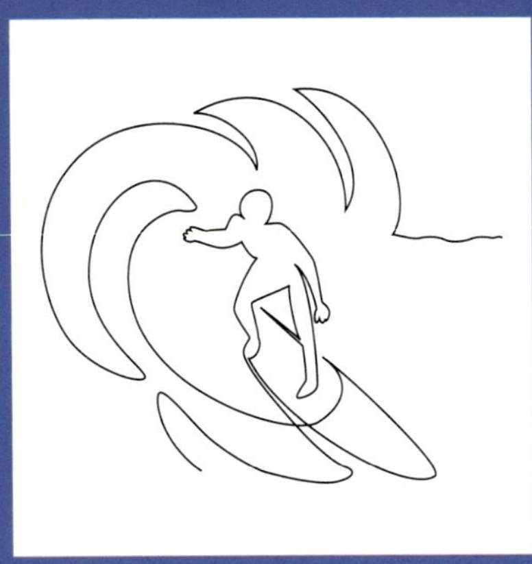

SPRING

I love you

SUMMER

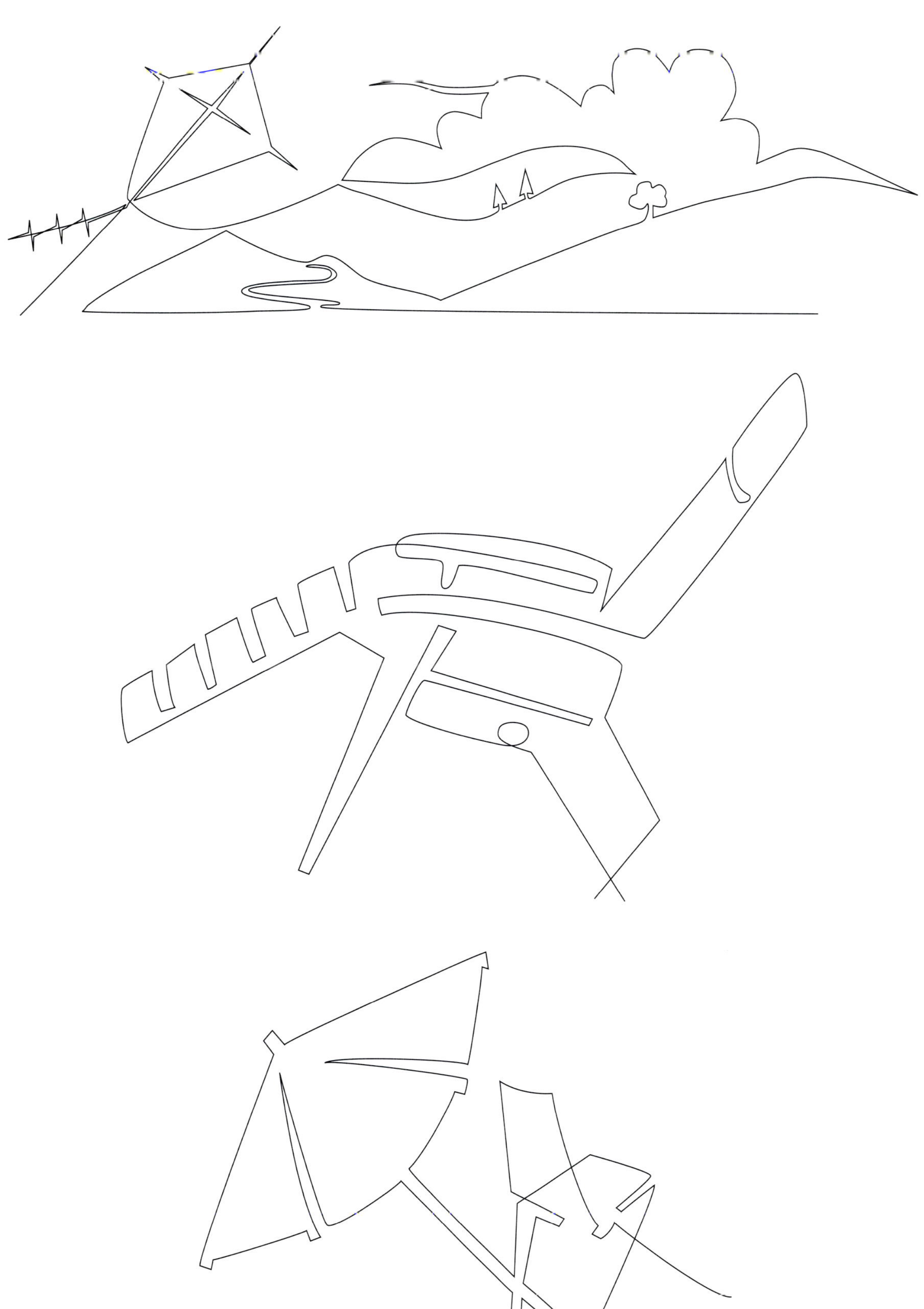

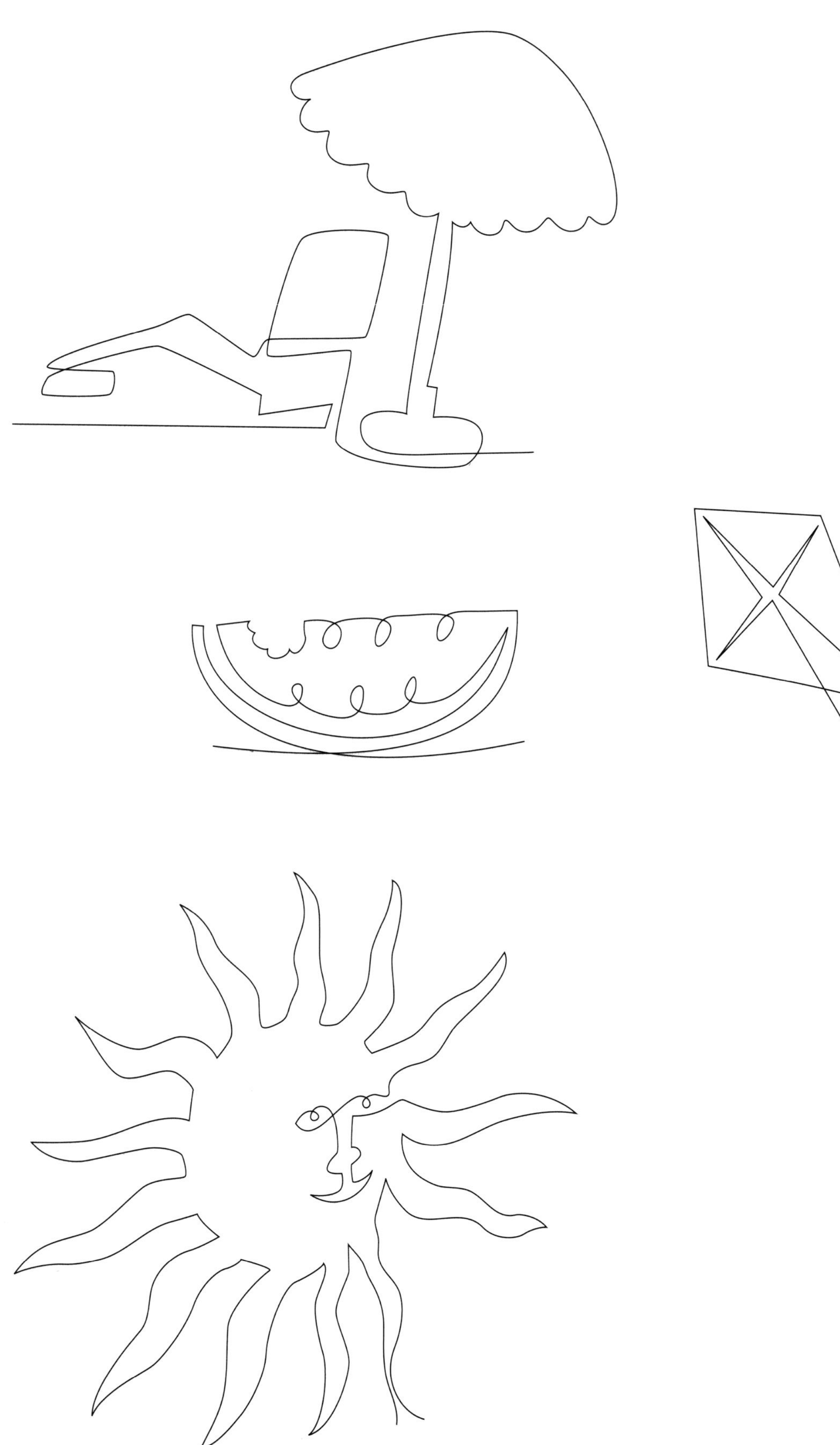

THROUGH THE SEASONS

FALL

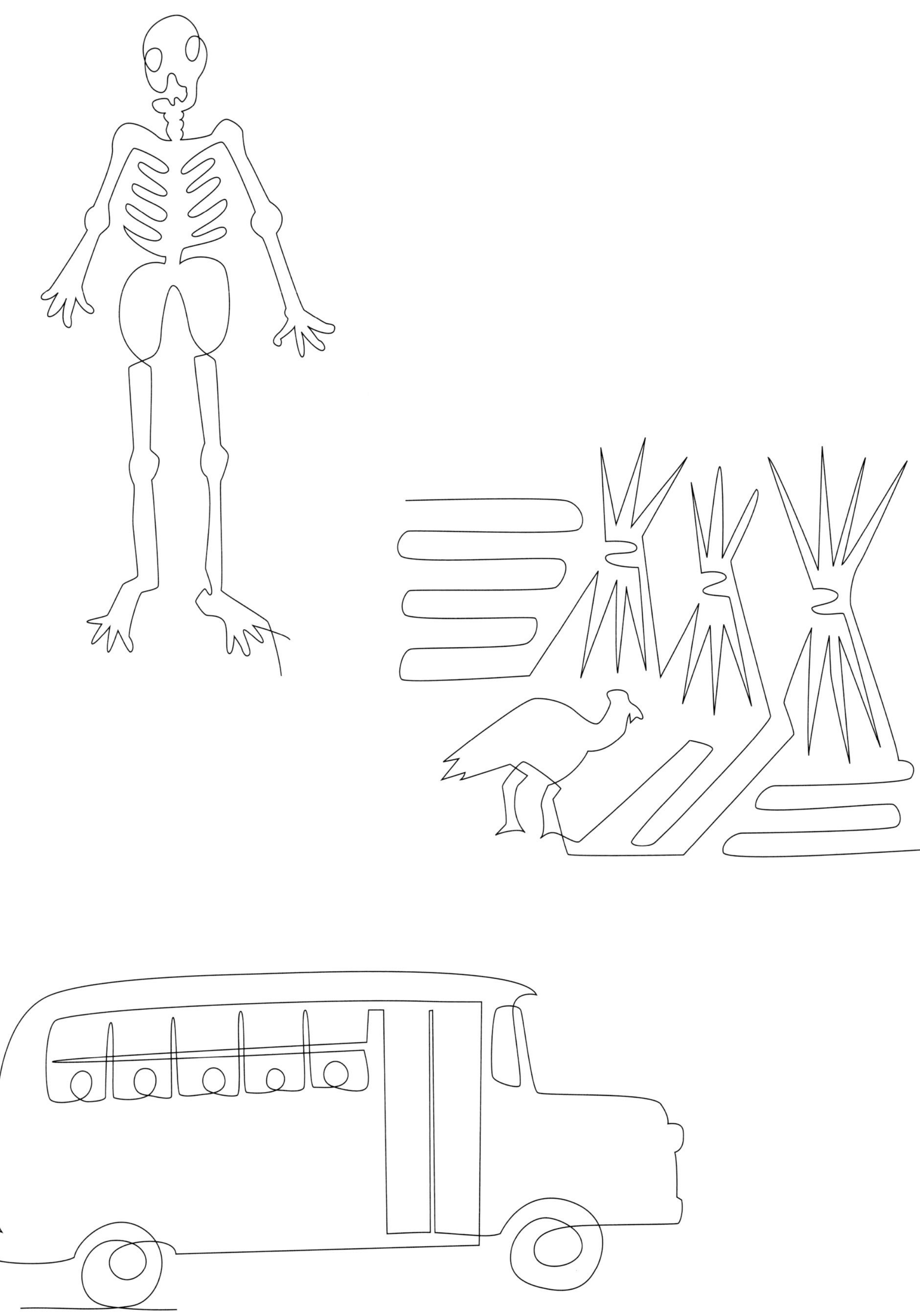

trick or treat

WINTER

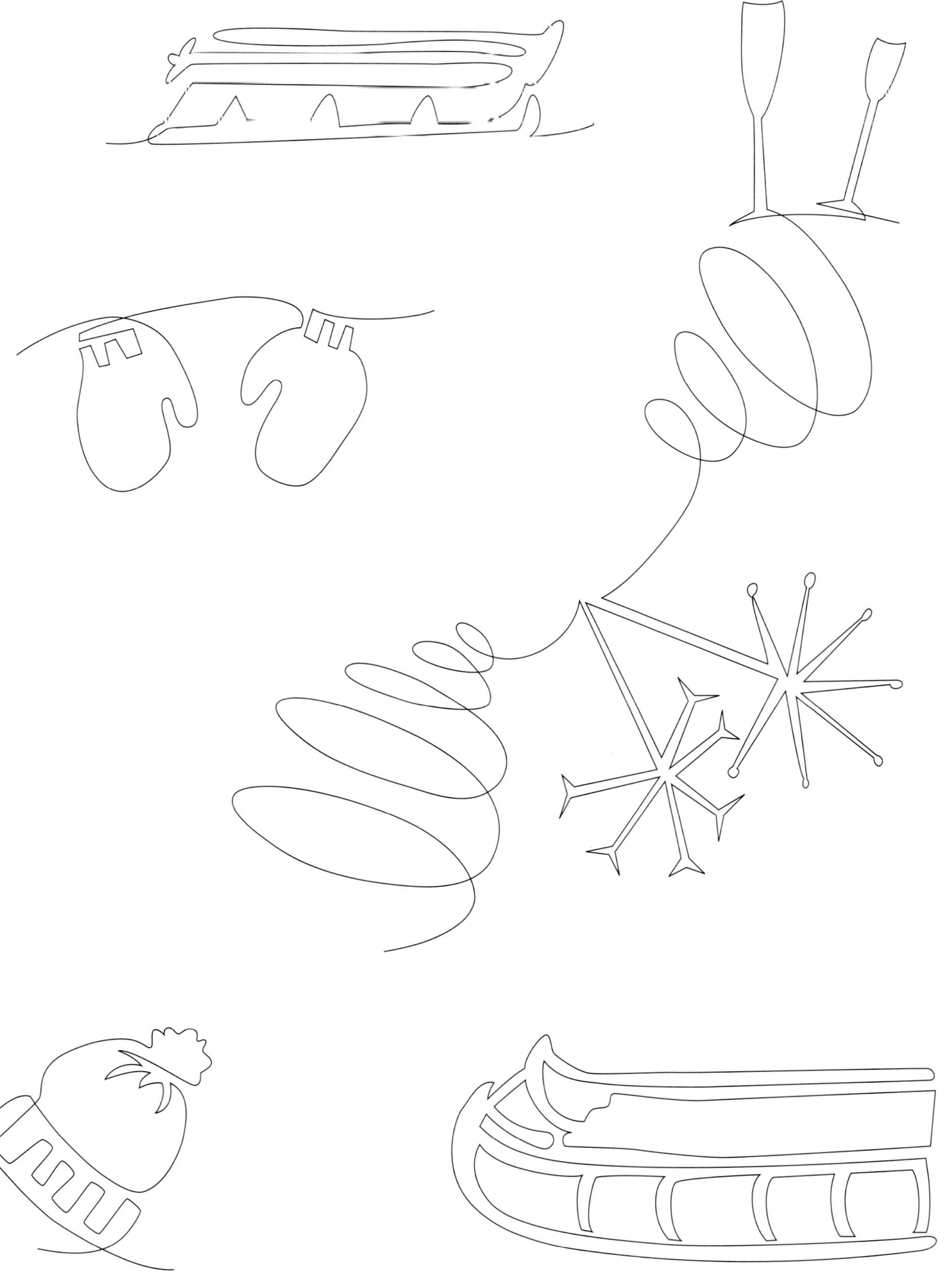

Globe Trotting

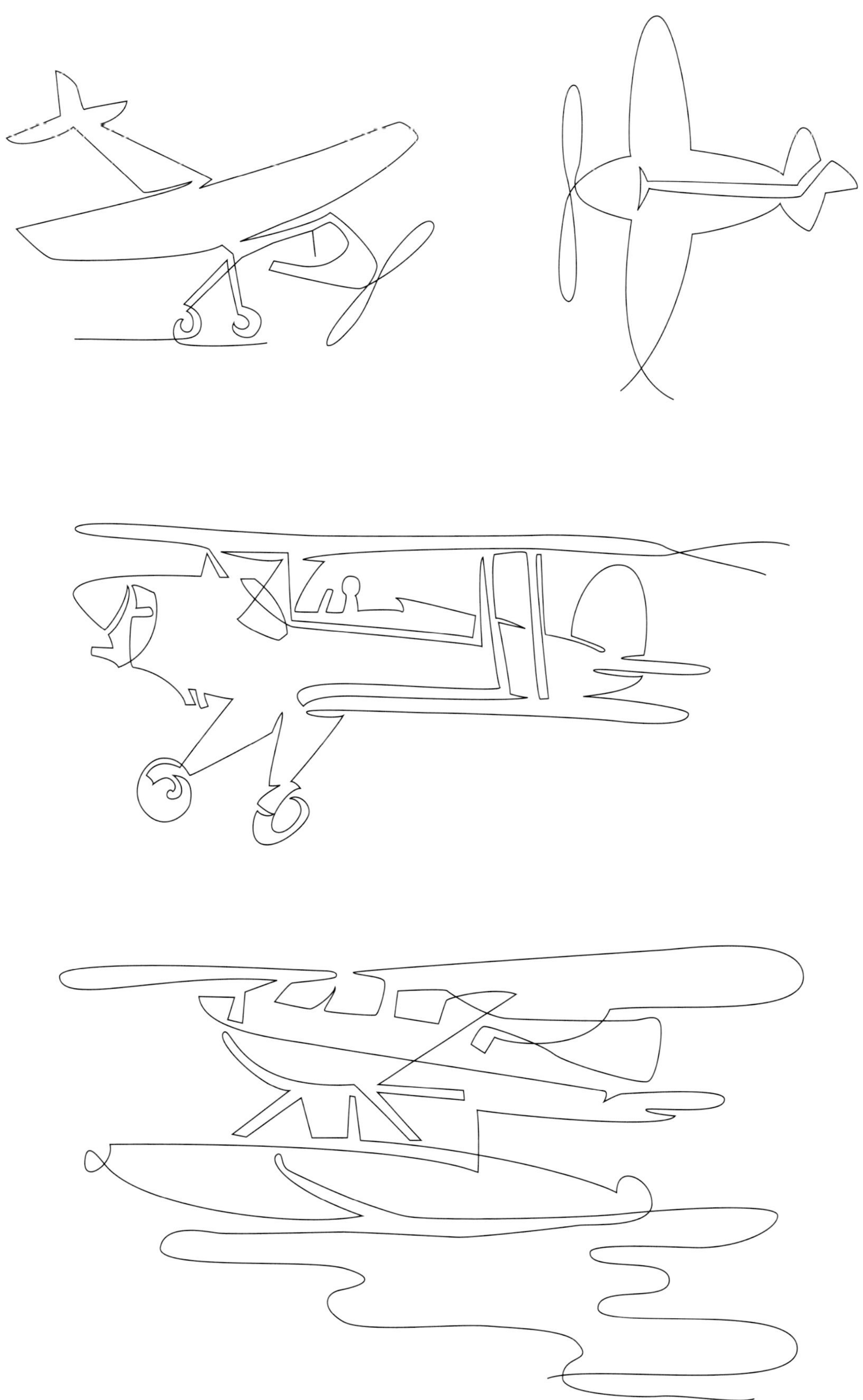

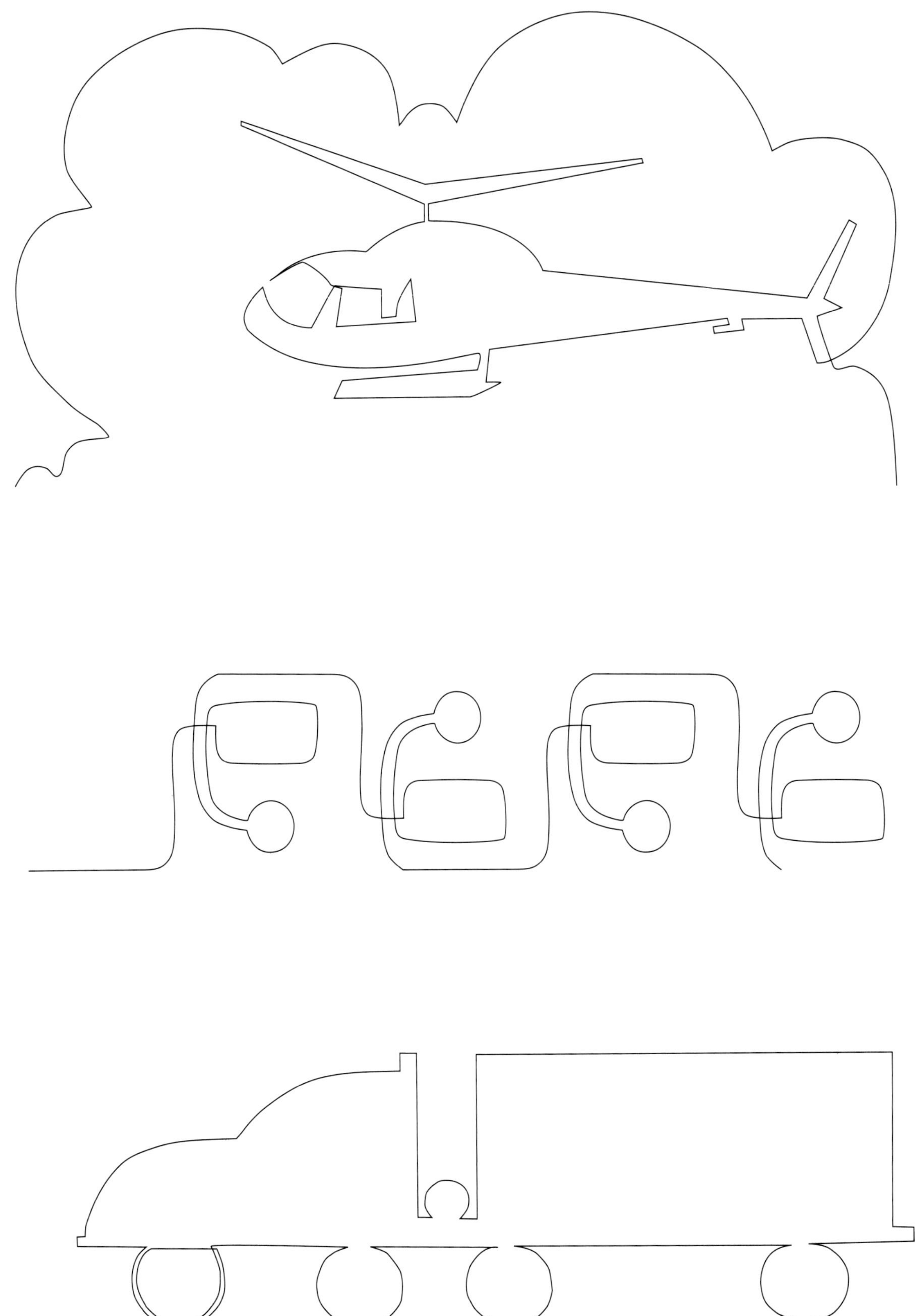

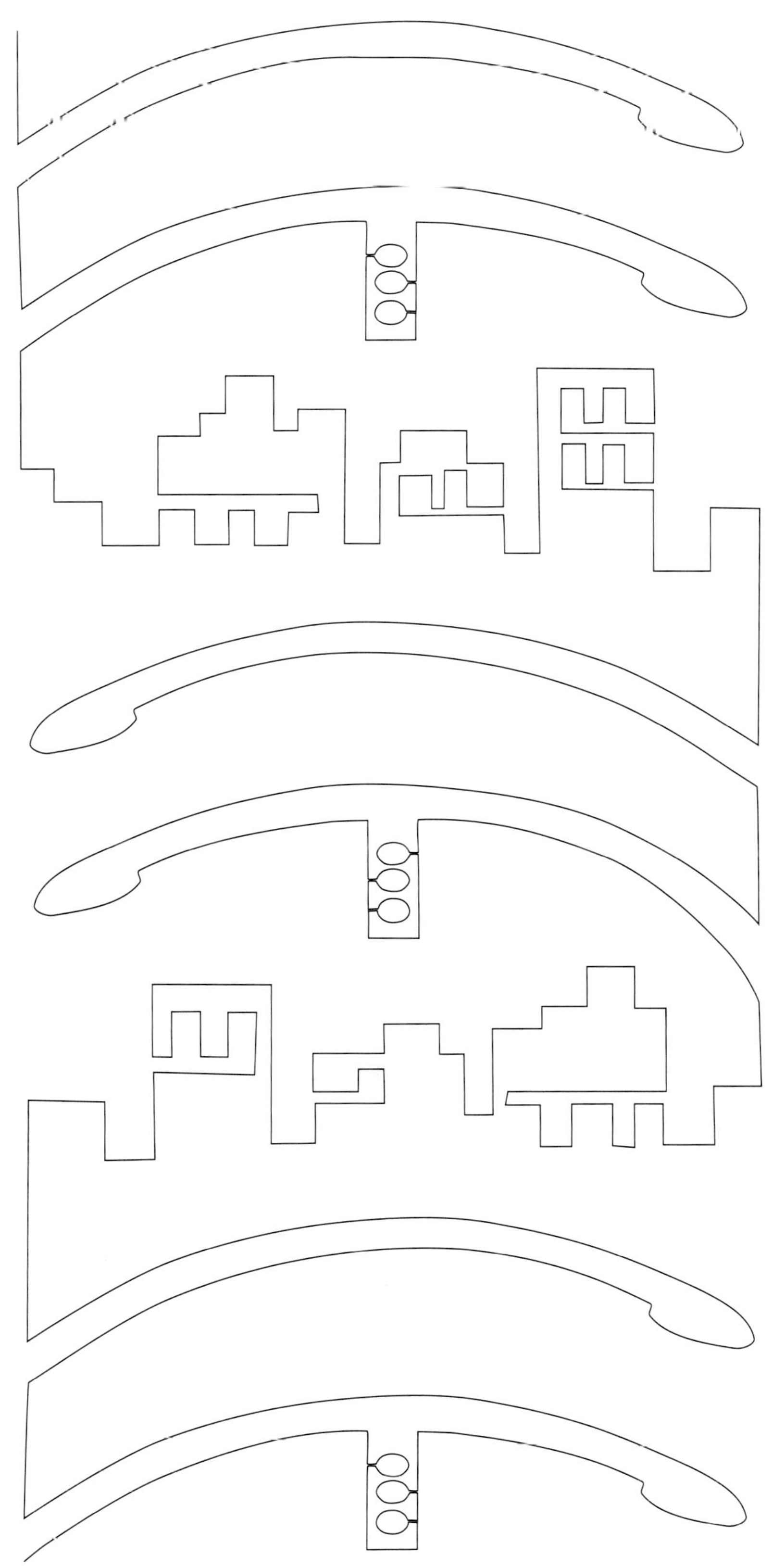

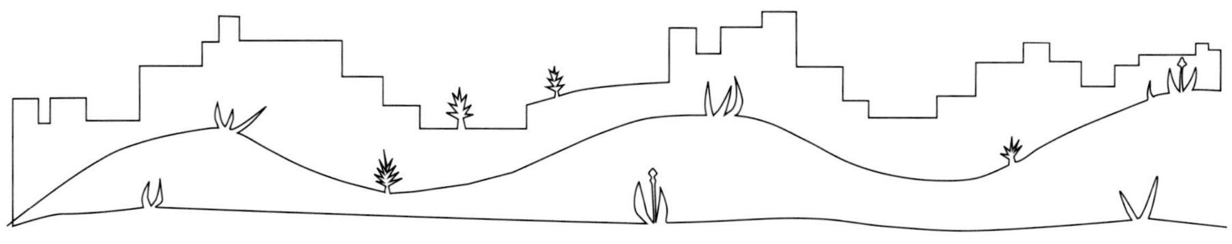

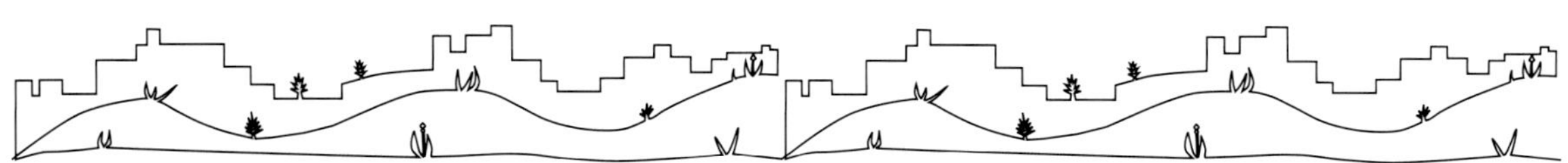

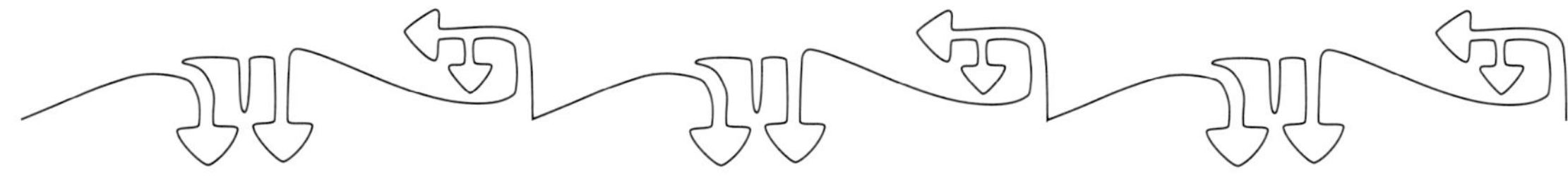

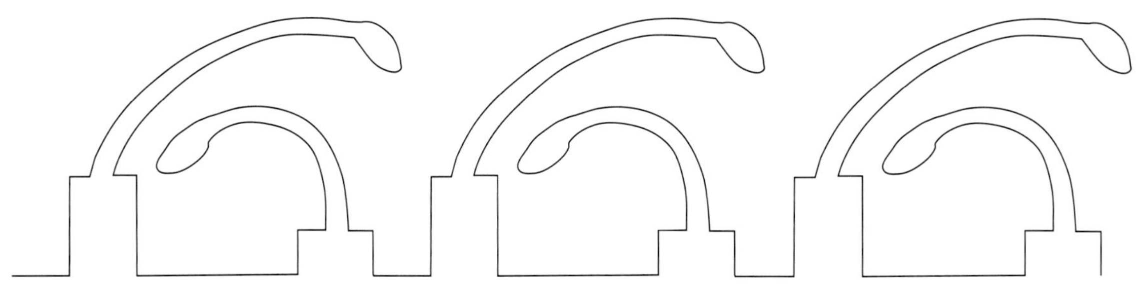

Out West

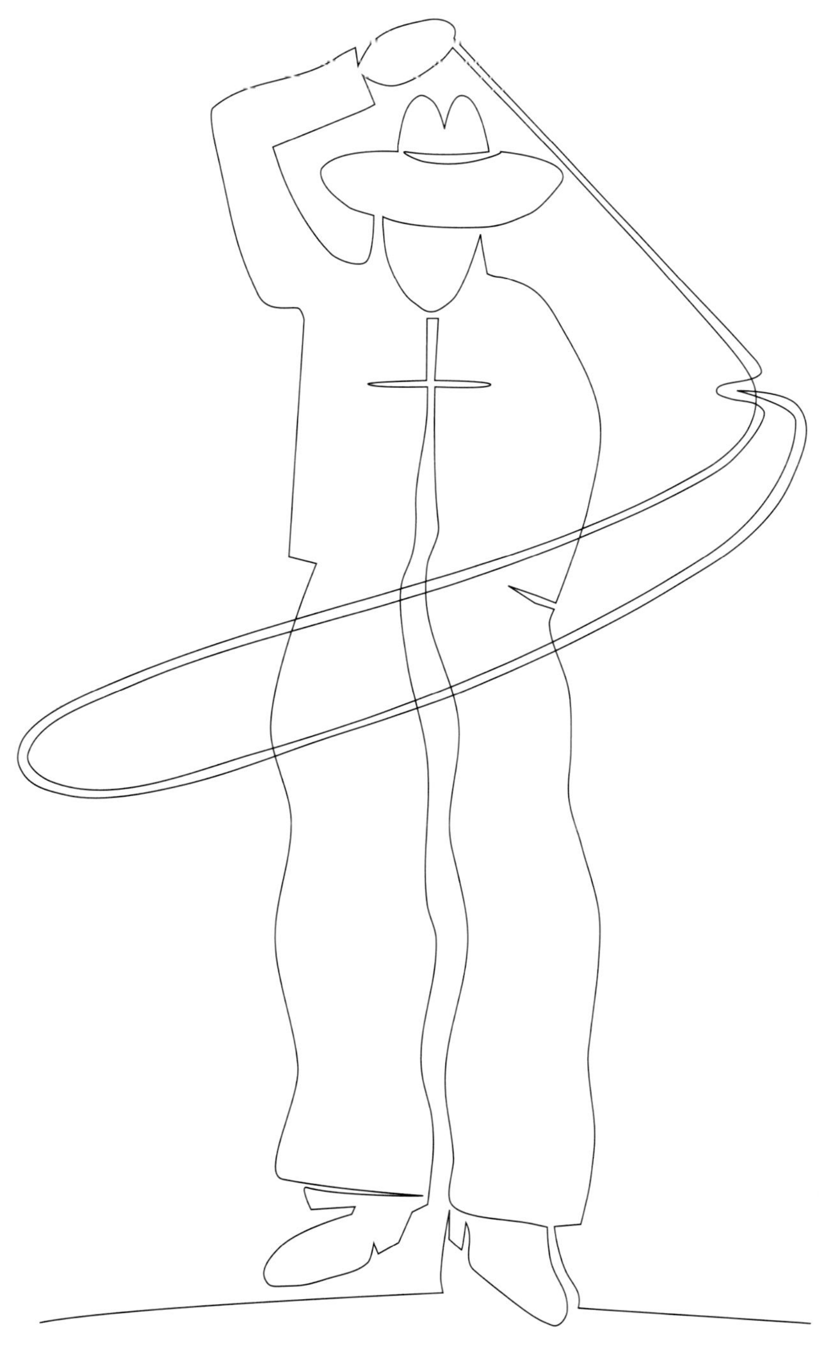

Entertainment

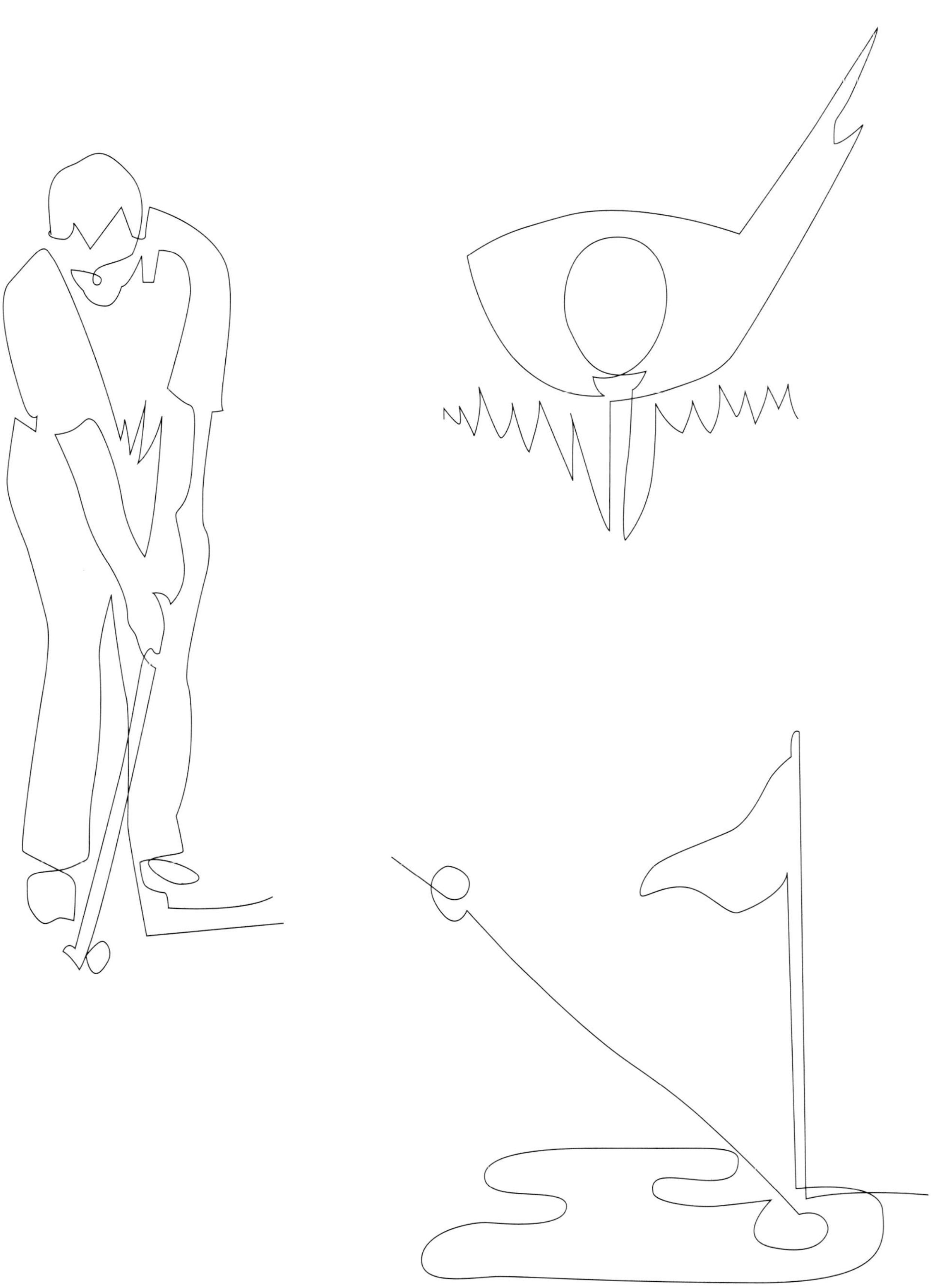

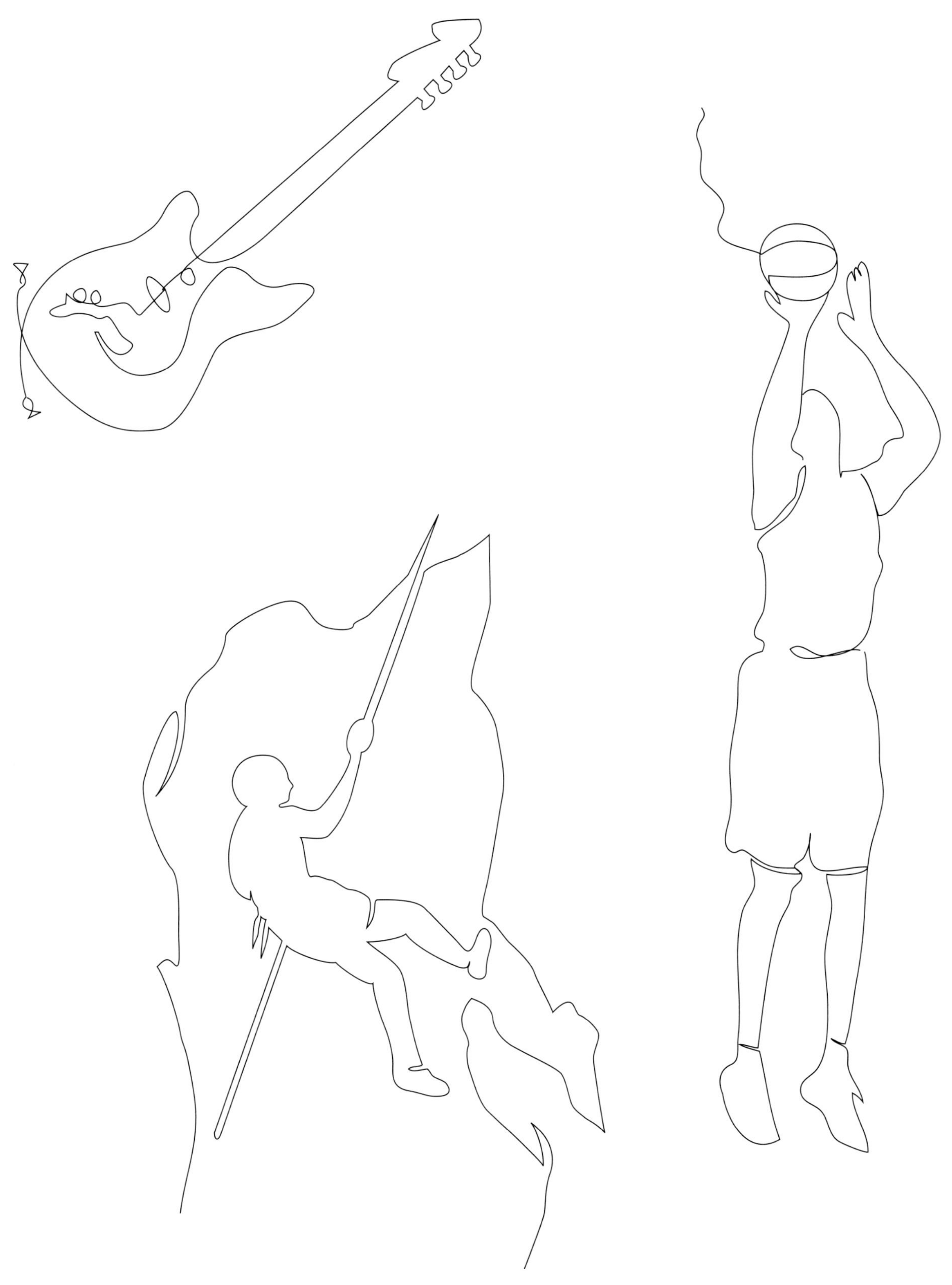

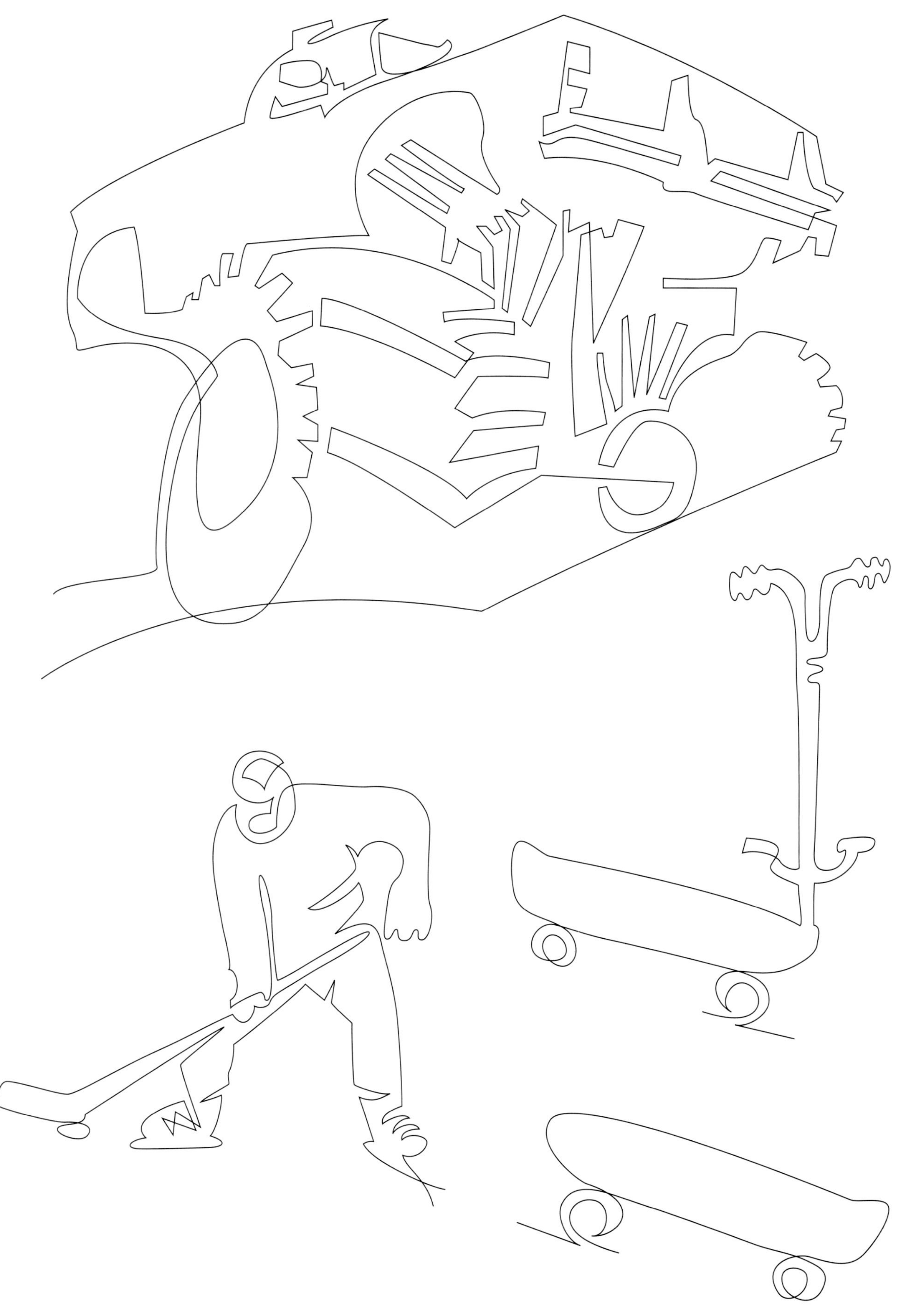

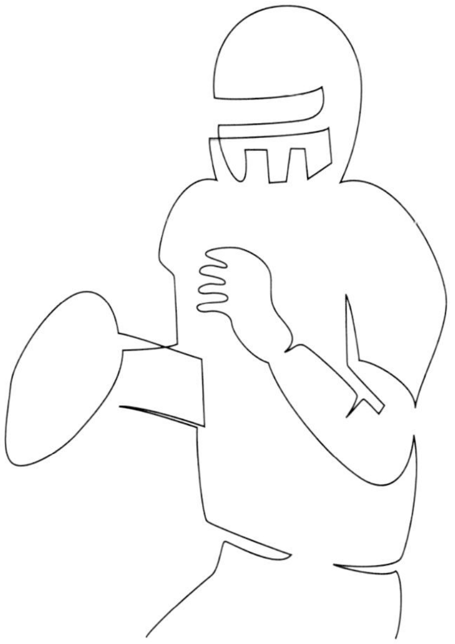

ENTERTAINMENT

Borders

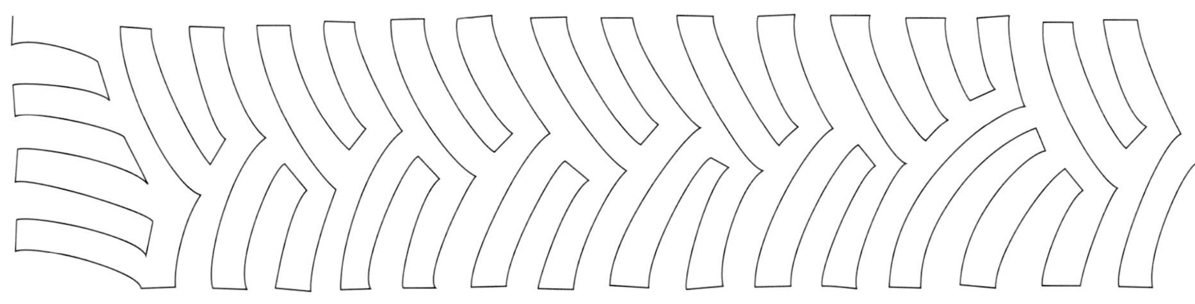

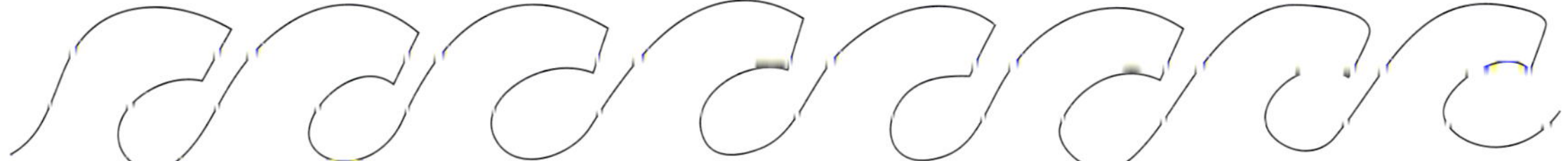

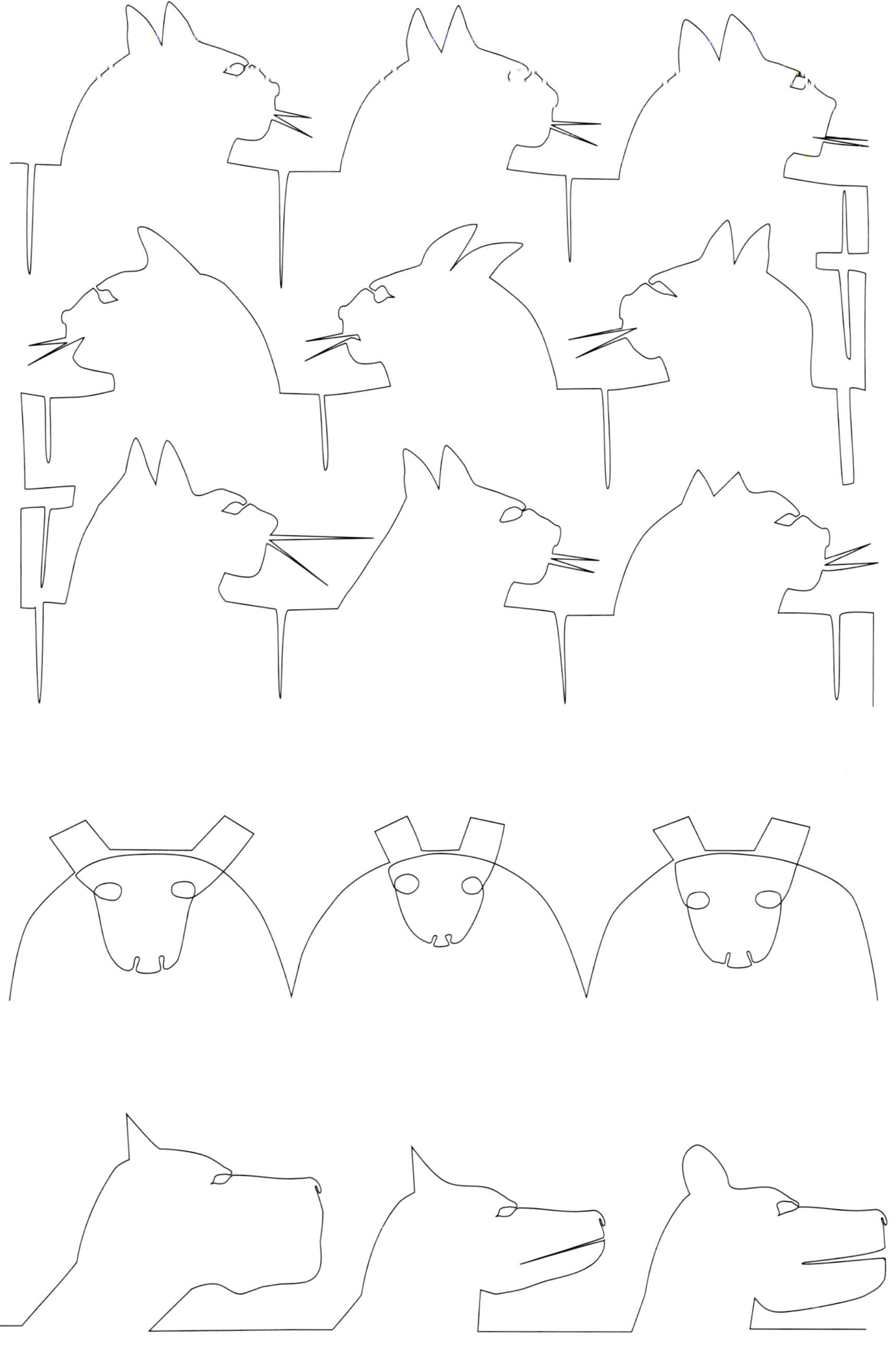

About the Author

Laura Lee Fritz is a practicing quiltmaker. Since 1989 she has been longarm quilting, teaching, and designing patterns for others to stitch. She draws images with personalities and relationships for you to compose into quilts that are more meaningful. From northern coastal California, Laura is inspired by living eye-to-eye with nature. Who takes a walk with whom? What entertains a duck? What does a pelican eat? Laura puts all this into continuous lines and fabric designs to make your quilt more exciting to make and to receive.

Laura has been a C&T author since 2000, with five titles of continuous-line design books, and also authored *The Art of Hand Appliqué* in 1989, from Schroeder Press. International Museum of Quilts and Textiles, and San Jose Museum of Quilts and Textiles both own Laura's quilts in their permanent collections.

Visit Laura online and follow on social media!

Website: lauraleefritz.net

Blog: lauraleefritz.net/blogs/news

Facebook: /lauraleefritzquilting

Instagram: @lauraleefritz

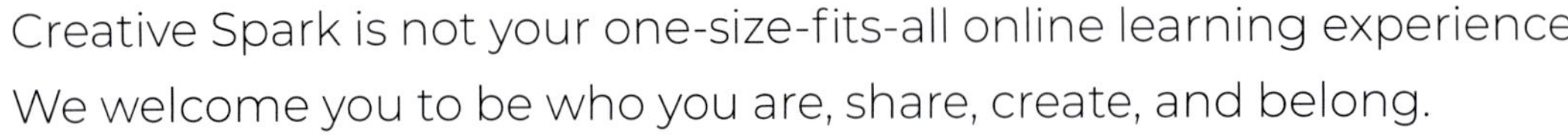